PRAISE FOR

THE VERSATILE LEADER

"There are many published books on leadership, but *The Versatile Leader* is one of a kind and stands out differently. Its structure is simple, attractive, and inspirational in many respects. I certainly recommend it. I have known Tese for nearly thirty years, and his authentic take on leadership resonates through every chapter. He has unpacked and shared his life lessons in this book with illustrations from day-to-day life. What's more, the references to African proverbs and scripture are delightful."

—JOSEPHINE FALADE
Pharmacist and lecturer, UCL School of Pharmacy
London, United Kingdom

"This business book is very engaging and authentic. As I read it, I realized that while working with Tese, I was learning about *The Versatile Leader* firsthand! What a privilege! The real-life events and examples bring home the points, making it easier for the reader to grasp the content. A considerable part of what I know today about leadership and management came from these teachings. Yet I know you did not clone me. Instead, you have prepared me well to be the successful businessman I am today. In addition, these principles have given me the confidence to handle, effectively, countless challenging situations. Thank you, Tese, for making such a significant impact on my career!"

—GUILHERME GUERRA
Managing partner, Consulang
Luanda, Angola

"*The Versatile Leader* reads like a novel with a rare combination of humor, practical life stories, and concepts that are easy to remember. Still, it has the capacity to completely alter the way you think and lead. By drawing from diverse contexts of life and business, you'll find a personal connection with it that will surprise you."

—BULUS SILAS BOSSAN
International vice president, The Navigators
Colorado Springs, Colorado, United States

"*The Versatile Leader* is a highly relevant and practical book for entrepreneurs. It was easy to read, and I found certain aspects particularly interesting. First, I enjoyed the African proverb starter for each chapter. It gave me perspective and increased my interest in what I was about to read. My favorite proverb is: 'A chameleon that wants to survive from the burning bush must abandon the majestic walk of its ancestors.' Second, the personal stories added more profound meaning to the book's message. Third, the author presented ideas that have been tested on the streets of life. Finally, this book has helped me appreciate the importance of the Bible in leadership."

—JONATHAN I. HUSSAINI
Founder, Globe Cabs Services
Abuja, Nigeria

"A handful of books have helped shape my perspective on life. I am honored to include *The Versatile Leader* as one of them. As an entrepreneur, husband, and father, I can find in the book nuggets of wisdom in every role I play and every season of my life. So, along with the Bible, I envision this book will become an essential handbook as I navigate the different seasons of business ownership."

—MAYAN MARSHALL
Co-owner, Uzima
Pittsburgh, Pennsylvania, United States

THE VERSATILE LEADER

THE VERSATILE LEADER

. . . .

THE CONFIDENCE
TO EXCEL
IN EVERY SITUATION

MSUEGA TESE

Forbes | Books

Published by Forbes Books, Charleston, South Carolina.
Member of Advantage Media.

Forbes Books is a registered trademark, and the Forbes Books colophon is a trademark of Forbes Media, LLC.

Printed in the United States of America.

10 9 8 7 6 5 4 3 2 1

ISBN: 978-1-955884-51-8 (Paperback)
ISBN: 978-1-955884-52-5 (eBook)

LCCN: 2022923665

Cover design by Matthew Morse.
Layout design by Matthew Morse.

All Scripture quotations, unless otherwise indicated, are taken from the Holy Bible, New International Version®, NIV®. Copyright ©1973, 1978, 1984, 2011 by Biblica, Inc.™ Used by permission of Zondervan. All rights reserved worldwide. www.zondervan.com The "NIV" and "New International Version" are trademarks registered in the United States Patent and Trademark Office by Biblica, Inc.™

This custom publication is intended to provide accurate information and the opinions of the author in regard to the subject matter covered. It is sold with the understanding that the publisher, Forbes Books, is not engaged in rendering legal, financial, or professional services of any kind. If legal advice or other expert assistance is required, the reader is advised to seek the services of a competent professional.

Since 1917, Forbes has remained steadfast in its mission to serve as the defining voice of entrepreneurial capitalism. Forbes Books, launched in 2016 through a partnership with Advantage Media, furthers that aim by helping business and thought leaders bring their stories, passion, and knowledge to the forefront in custom books. Opinions expressed by Forbes Books authors are their own. To be considered for publication, please visit **books.Forbes.com**.

To my mother, Mama Mtom.
Your sacrificial love means so much to me.
Thank you!

CONTENTS

PART I
FOUNDATION

PART II
STRATEGY

ACKNOWLEDGMENTS

I am glad my late father would allow me to listen to the deliberations of the village elders at a young age. It has become the backbone of my leadership journey. I am also very thankful to Dominic and Chidi Ichaba for introducing me to the concept of leadership metaphors that transformed me into a lifelong student of leadership.

Initially, I had planned to take chunks of time off to write. However, I soon realized that wasn't necessary, as I have a brilliant team of writers at home. As usual, my wife, Mhide, remained very understanding and supportive. As I wrote, my children—Sefa, Sena, Sensha, Vater, and Civir—provided helpful critiques and inputs. My sister, Lamen, verified our childhood events and made other contributions to the manuscript. I love every one of you.

I'm grateful to those of you who have contributed to my growth and development since childhood. Unfortunately, there is not enough space here to name all of you. The motherly love and support of Mama Christine Filipe and the late Mama Hunda Makurdi made a tremendous difference in my life.

I sincerely thank my high school teachers, Mr. Nder Kuhwa and Mr. George Varghese. You guided me well. I appreciate Dr. Chris Oliobi and the late Mrs. Chi Oliobi for modeling what they taught me. Biodun AkanbiOluwa and John Gardner, I can't thank you enough for contributing immensely to my career in information technology. I also express my gratitude to Reverend João César. Your friendship and prayers have given me great encouragement over the last two decades. My heartfelt thanks to Pastors Romão and Luciana Meto. You lead in selfless service to others. Dr. Edward and Kate Fynn, you have been great friends. Eddie and Sandra Brown, you have shown me the importance of accountability. Thank you.

I thank my colleagues at Integrated Solutions Angola, Vallantis, and E360. You have endured my shortcomings and contributed significantly to what we have achieved so far. For a long time, many people who heard me speak about leadership insisted that I write a book. Your confidence in me has been a source of motivation. I am appreciative of the participants who offered valuable insights at my seminars. You have greatly enriched *The Versatile Leader*.

Many people, such as Lynn Lipschitz, Irene Webba, Maria Ambrosio, Felix Okot, and Taiwo Oluyomi, read the manuscript and furnished valuable comments. I owe every one of you a debt of gratitude. To everyone who provided the testimonials, I take your words with gratitude, humility, and responsibility. I am very grateful to William Adelekan for thoroughly reviewing the manuscript and writing the foreword with exceptional insight.

The publisher, Forbes Books, has an excellent team of professionals. Working with you has been such a pleasant experience. Your positive attitude and timely support brought this dream to reality. I am particularly indebted to Ezra Byer, Samantha Miller, Matthew Morse, Laura Rashley, Heath Ellison, Olivia Tanksley, and Natasha Walstra.

Lastly, I am exceedingly thankful to God, who gave me the dream, provided everything, and brought the right people into my life to help make this contribution.

I pray that this book will help produce more leaders who will improve our world by leading with authenticity, confidence, and excellence.

FOREWORD

I am privileged to write the foreword to this interesting book, *The Versatile Leader*, by my friend and brother in Christ, Msuega Tese. I first met Msuega in 2010 when I was a team leader in Eni Angola, in Luanda. During my time in Luanda (2010 to 2017), he served creditably in various leadership positions in our church, Angola International Christian Church. He demonstrated impressive leadership skills in the church environment. In addition, he experienced firsthand the leadership principles outlined in this book as someone who cofounded a successful information technology services company in Angola.

The Versatile Leader gives a refreshing approach to this very important subject. Despite reading many books and attending many seminars on leadership, it was not easy for the author to find a definition of leadership that appealed to him. However, the definition given by Professor Robert Steven Kaplan was just what he was looking for. According to Professor Kaplan, "Leadership is figuring out your beliefs and having the guts/ability to act on them in such a way that adds value to others." The author appropriately summarized this definition with the following keywords: beliefs, actions, and benefits.

The author defined a versatile leader as "a person of integrity who, along with others, creates valued outcomes using appropriate metaphors." He pointed out the importance of switching to appropriate metaphors with integrity when the situation under consideration changes. He asserted that "success will elude us if the situation changes and we don't adapt our leadership." This is in line with this Namibian proverb he quoted: "When the rhythm of the drumbeat changes, the dance steps must adapt."

I particularly like the following aspects of the book:

- The subject of leadership presented in an interesting, engaging writing style and important principles conveyed in a way that is easy to understand
- Use of familiar occupations as metaphors to drive home important aspects of strategy and tactics
- References to Bible verses/stories/principles to emphasize some important points
- References to lessons learned from the author's dad and his workplace
- The author's frankness and humility that come across in this book (he referred to personal stories to illustrate where he was wrong and identified important lessons learned)
- Use of relevant African proverbs (from Nigeria, Angola, Namibia, Uganda, etc.)
- Inclusion of an example in the last chapter showing how some of the principles in the book can be applied

I am convinced that *The Versatile Leader* will be very valuable to leaders and those who aspire to be leaders in various walks of life. I highly recommend this book to you all.

—WILLIAM A. ADELEKAN
Chorley, Lancashire, United Kingdom
November 2022

INTRODUCTION

A good beginning is of no value unless one perseveres to the end.
—NIGERIAN PROVERB

I shall never forget the year 1997. I got married during the first quarter of that year. Some months later, the promotion to become a supervisor at work came. Unfortunately, I had a poor start in both roles! Thankfully, I had a mentor who guided me in the right direction. What he did with me stirred up my interest and transformed me into a lifelong student of leadership. Since then, I have read more books than I can name and have attended many seminars to reinforce my leadership skills. Moreover, I constantly analyze news and events through the lens of leadership. Over time, I observed that many of the challenges people face in different areas of life are interlinked.

Leadership skills are needed everywhere. Unfortunately, only certain people in need do have them. However, it is possible to overcome this shortcoming and become a versatile leader if desired. I define a versatile leader as a person of integrity who, along with others, creates valued outcomes using appropriate metaphors. The principles you are about to learn are very portable. You can use them anywhere with no need for retooling.

Initially, I taught my friends and colleagues these principles. With time, the scope expanded to facilitating leadership seminars in different settings, such as businesses, churches, and associations. The feedback, in addition to my experience, has helped to refine these crucial lessons. As you are about to see, the scope of what I have discovered is broad. However, I have carefully structured these principles to help readers remember them easily and lead confidently, regardless of the context.

STRUCTURE

The structure of this book is as follows. Part I provides the foundation for the subsequent parts. Chapter 1 examines the definition of leadership that conveys my underlying thoughts. Chapters 2 and 3 also form part of the foundation and cover fundamental concepts, including situational leadership, metaphors, and the organizational life cycle, also referred to as the S-Curve.

Each chapter in parts II and III presents an occupation used as a metaphor. The first part of each chapter describes the context, and the remaining sections amplify the relevant qualities of the metaphor.

Part II contains metaphors for less frequent actions called strategy. You may not need these metaphors every day, yet their impact is profound. They set the stage for tactics, the metaphors in part III. The starting point for this section is the physician metaphor. When you get into a new leadership situation, this metaphor will help you make a diagnosis. Then, you will decide on the next steps.

Depending on what you have discovered, you may use architect, builder, or engineer as an implementation metaphor. The architect metaphor helps articulate the vision for your new organization. If you join a company that is healthy and ready to grow, you can execute its existing vision like a builder. An existential threat to an organization requires an engineer for its turnaround. Irrespective of the context, the leader must deliver expected results the way entrepreneurs do.

Part III relates to tactics. These are metaphors you will frequently use in pursuit of your goals. Obtaining reliable information on an ongoing basis demands the skills of a journalist. That is where to start. Essentially, the journalist metaphor does for tactics what the physician does for strategy. The remaining six metaphors are equally divided to cover internal and external settings.

The internal tactical metaphors are coach, parent, and judge. Use these metaphors where your authority is not in doubt. When you need to train your team, be the coach. The parent metaphor is best when considering the long-term implication of your action. Be fair to each party when conflict arises, like a good judge.

The external tactical metaphors—pilot, soldier, and diplomat—will help when you lack authority or control. Thinking like a pilot will give you confidence when handling emergencies. In tough situations, you will need the discipline and courage of a soldier. Finally, the tact of a diplomat will help in sensitive circumstances.

These metaphors enable a leader to adapt to various situations authentically.

The final section, part IV, consists of just two chapters. Chapter 16 provides essential elements, such as adaptability and humility, that enable the leader to work seamlessly with others. If you are wondering how to begin applying the lessons learned, please start with chapter 17. Then, if you start well, you can stand out from the crowd.

CROWDED

At the time of this writing, over sixty thousand leadership books are available on Amazon. Sixty thousand! Many say the field is very crowded, which begs the question, *Why must I write yet another book on leadership?* I have some answers to this question.

First, I'm not afraid of crowds. I once lived in Lagos, a Nigerian city with an estimated 21 million inhabitants. It is the largest urban center in Africa and is infamous for its traffic jams. I had to pass through Oshodi every day to and from work. If you're unfamiliar with the area, the population density of Oshodi is seven times that of Lagos itself! That does not include the multitude that transits through its overcrowded bus stop.[1]

Nevertheless, Oshodi didn't scare or prevent me from pursuing the career I cherished. I knew where I was going, and the multitude did not deter me. Like myself, each person was making their journey. Similarly, despite the numerous books on leadership, *The Versatile Leader* brings a fresh perspective that many readers will find helpful.

Second, allow me a moment to *debrief.* From childhood and growing up in a rural community, my dad often said, "Listen while you play."

He would say this as the other elders arrived and then send me, along with the other kids, out of the village reception hut.[2] It meant that we would play quietly nearby while the adults were discussing different subjects.

When the elders left, my dad would call us back into the hut to report what each child had heard and learned. Those sessions made a

---

1   CityFacts.com, "Oshodi-Isolo," accessed November 14, 2022, https://www.city-facts.com/oshodi-isolo.

2   This is known among the Tiv people as *Áte*, although many other Africans call it *Jango*.

tremendous impact on me. To this day, my father's voice echoes in my mind: "Listen while you play." After over fifty years of "listening," I finally consider it the right moment to debrief. I believe all readers will find the lessons I have learned beneficial.

I often wondered why the adults in my village didn't mind that children sent out of the hut were playing in its vicinity. The reason was simple. The elders used so many parables that it was difficult for children to understand even if they listened carefully. Although we couldn't grasp everything, we would pick up an adage that would elate us. Those proverbs were insightful, and some were entertaining. As I grew, my interest in them increased. I have now accumulated quite a number of these wise sayings—one of which you will find at the start of each chapter. Not intending to confuse anyone, I have selected those that bring out the central message of each chapter, which a diverse audience can understand.

To this day, my father's voice echoes in my mind: "Listen while you play."

Third, despite the many books on leadership, finding suitable leaders remains a significant challenge to organizations. Without good leaders, society is in trouble. Every family needs at least one leader. Since it is difficult to count how many families are in the world, we'll try something else. Every team of twenty soccer players (including reserves) usually has at least one leader, the coach. Assuming the 8 billion people in the world today are divided into teams of twenty each, you will get 400 million teams—each requiring a leader. Considering this significant number, the sixty thousand leadership books on Amazon suddenly feel like a small number!

EVERYONE

Occasionally, every person will find themselves in a situation where leadership skills could help them stand out. The insights from *The Versatile Leader* will help you become more assertive in handling many challenges—even if you don't want to be called a leader.

As a technologist and a businessman, I recognize my own biases. As such, people involved in business may find my examples familiar. Yet the ideas I present are generic, and anyone in any leadership situation can find them helpful. You will also see that my Christian faith has considerably shaped my views. That said, I do not presume that readers are familiar with the biblical texts I have used. In addition, you do not need to know the Bible beforehand to benefit from this book.

In general, I set out to offer easy-to-remember practical skills so readers can confidently deal with various leadership challenges. In addition, I aim to assist new leaders in mastering these crucial concepts in the shortest time possible. Experienced leaders may also find in *The Versatile Leader* a practical framework that will significantly simplify their decision-making process.

Finally, as Nigerians wisely say, "A good beginning is of no value unless one perseveres to the end." I'm optimistic that you will find *The Versatile Leader* insightful, refreshing, and helpful as you read to the very end. Families, communities, companies, churches, countries, and the world desperately need versatile leaders.

PART I

FOUNDATION

CHAPTER 1

DEFINITION

When you pray, move your feet.
—WEST AFRICAN PROVERB

WHAT IS LEADERSHIP?

Joseph Clarence Rost, professor of leadership, analyzed hundreds of leadership definitions offered by authors in the twentieth century. In 1991, he published his findings in a book titled *Leadership for the Twenty-First Century*. One of his conclusions was that "the dictionary definitions of leadership have been, and continue to be, very simple and, as a result, are not very helpful in understanding the concept." Furthermore, Rost anticipated that "leadership scholars in the future are going to have to think new thoughts about leadership … critically analyze one another's theories and models, and engage in dialogic conversations about those conceptual frameworks."[3]

---

3   Joseph C. Rost, *Leadership for the Twenty-First Century* (Westport, CT: Praeger, February 18, 1993).

Professor Rost is not the only one who observed the challenges of defining leadership. Professor Robert Steven Kaplan also noted, "If I asked a hundred people to define leadership, I would probably get a hundred different answers."[4] Please be aware that Kaplan taught leadership at Harvard Business School.

However, what is exciting is that Kaplan has defined leadership in a way that makes perfect sense. Consequently, I have ended the many years of my search for a definition of leadership. I vividly remember my first day attending the Harvard Business School leadership class in 2013. Professor Kaplan started his lecture with this statement: "Leadership is figuring out your beliefs and having the guts/ability to act on them in such a way that adds value to others."[5]

I like this way of looking at leadership because it contains three critical components that are very appropriate. First, you want to start by figuring out your beliefs. Beliefs are in the spotlight whenever there is a contemplation of purpose or other vital questions of life. Therefore, clarifying yours is an excellent place to start as a leader. Second, you need to act on those beliefs. Knowing your beliefs is nice, but more is required. You must put them into action to be called a leader. Third, a leader must add value to others. This is where we evaluate leadership. It's ensuring your actions are producing positive results for others.

We can summarize Kaplan's definition with these three words: beliefs, actions, and benefits.

---

4   Robert Steven Kaplan, *What You're Really Meant to Do* (Boston, MA: Harvard Business Review Press, May 7, 2013).

5   Harvard Business School OPM46 class notes, May 2013.

BELIEFS

Beliefs have profound implications on individuals as well as organizations. Thomas J. Watson Jr., the former CEO of IBM, wrote:

> Consider any great organization—one that has lasted over the years—and I think you will find that it owes its resiliency, not to its form of organization or administrative skills, but to the power of what we call beliefs and the appeal these beliefs have for its people … I firmly believe that any organization, in order to survive and achieve success, must have a sound set of beliefs on which it premises all its policies and actions. Next, I believe that the most important single factor in corporate success is faithful adherence to those beliefs.[6]

Countries, empires, and even civilizations are built and destroyed on beliefs. In his book *Civilization: The West and the Rest*, Niall Ferguson, a Scottish historian, argued that the rise of Western civilization is a product of Protestant work ethics. A belief about work, wealth, and education spurred actions that inspired Europe to world dominance for many centuries. Unfortunately, as Europeans have become complacent, they "work less; they also pray less—and believe less." As a result, their dominance has waned.[7]

Even though whole civilizations are created with beliefs, they are deeply personal. Former president of Nigeria Olusegun Obasanjo said, "A man is a slave to his belief[s] because he will unconsciously do everything in his power to conform to them."[8] Therefore, we need to

---

6   Thomas J. Watson Jr., *A Business and Its Beliefs* (New York: McGraw-Hill, 2003).

7   Niall Ferguson, *Civilization* (New York: Penguin Publishing Group, 2011), 266.

8   Olusegun Obasanjo, *This Animal Called Man* (ALF Publications, 1998).

ensure that what we are conforming our lives to is not causing harm to others but is beneficial to society.

Examining one's beliefs is an exercise not just for the philosopher or the clergy. Every person should attempt to answer fundamental questions, such as "Where do we come from? What are we? Where are we going?"[9] Interestingly, these three questions are the title of a famous painting found in the Museum of Fine Arts in Boston, Massachusetts. It is an early twentieth-century work of the French artist Paul Gauguin. The painting contains a beach scene of people, animals, and plants, with the sea and hills in the background.

We need to ensure that what we are conforming our lives to is not causing harm to others but is beneficial to society.

However, no one would seriously agree that Gauguin's or any other artwork can answer these profound questions. Os Guinness, the author of *The Great Quest*, wrote:

> The truth is that the urgent need of our times is a fresh seriousness about human existence and a renewed openness to ultimate questions. Answers to ultimate questions are not only vital to each of us as individuals but to whole societies and civilizations. Indeed, there are no great societies or civilizations without confident answers to ultimate questions, and such answers need to become vital again in our schools, our universities, and our public discussion as well as in our families.[10]

---

9   Peter Russell, *Delphi Complete Works of Paul Gauguin (Illustrated)* (East Sussex, UK: Delphi Classics, December 8, 2016).

10   Os Guinness, *The Great Quest* (Westmont, IL: IVP, March 22, 2022).

Guinness outlined a four-step approach that helps everyone tackle this crucial quest. The steps are questions, answers, evidence, and commitment. Leadership will be pointless without a sense of purpose. Therefore, I urge every leader to take personal responsibility and address these primary questions head-on. After this, however, you can act confidently.

ACTIONS

Without action, beliefs are of no value. James, one of the early church leaders, asked the rhetorical question, "You foolish person, do you want evidence that faith without deeds is useless?"[11] James further argued that Israel's ancestors, such as Abraham and Isaac, became faith heroes because of their actions. If we look around us, we will also find many good examples of people who acted on their beliefs for the well-being of others. Sonya Carson is one such example.

In 2009, a movie called *Gifted Hands* told the story of US presidential candidate and neurosurgeon Ben Carson, who would eventually serve as the seventeenth US Secretary of Housing and Urban Development.[12] The significant part of Carson's story was the role his mother, Sonya, played in his life. Married at just thirteen years of age, divorced, and only possessing a third-grade education, she didn't even know how to read. She was a housemaid and lived in abject poverty. Still, she had a simple but essential belief: "Learn to do your best. God will do the rest."[13]

Instead of sitting down, crying, and feeling sorry for herself, she acted on what she believed. She wanted her kids to have a better life,

---

11 James 2:20.

12 *Gifted Hands: The Ben Carson Story*, directed by Thomas Carter (Sony Pictures Television, 2009), https://www.imdb.com/title/tt1295085/.

13 *Gifted Hands: The Ben Carson Story,* https://www.imdb.com/title/tt1295085/.

so she reduced their TV time and insisted they go to the library and read. Ben Carson would become an internationally admired figure because her actions gave him a firm foundation. We can learn from Sonya that, regardless of the situation in which a leader finds herself, she must act according to what she believes to be true. For without action, there can be no benefits.

BENEFITS

While it is not wrong to think of the personal gain one can derive from a situation, a leader should always focus on what will be helpful to others. Very often, a leader makes some form of personal sacrifice to enrich the lives of others. This is normal and expected. However, if someone imposes sacrifice on one group so others will reap the benefits, this is no longer leadership—especially if this person is not part of the sacrifice. The old saying goes, "You cannot rob Mario to pay Maria."

A great example of a leader who acted consistently on his beliefs for the benefit of others is the biblical character Joseph. This young man was sold into slavery because he was his father's favorite. Despite this misfortune, Joseph excelled wherever he found himself.

When he worked at the house of an Egyptian official named Potiphar, he did so with diligence. Potiphar's wife pursued him tirelessly, but he would not flirt with her. Consequently, they locked him up. Even in jail, Joseph was kind and cared for other inmates. Eventually, he became second in command over all of Egypt. If he had strayed from his values, he could have become very corrupt, but he was upright. When he had a chance to repay his brothers, who had been cruel to him, he didn't. Instead, he said to them, "And now, do not be distressed and do not be angry with yourselves for selling me here because it was to save lives that God sent me ahead of you."[14] Wherever he turned he acted with integrity and helped others, ultimately saving Egypt and surrounding nations from a severe food shortage that lasted for seven years.

This is my understanding of authentic leadership. It is consistently acting on your beliefs for the benefit of others. Whether you are at the top or bottom of any organizational chart, your integrity remains a constant. Even if sidelined and mistreated, you can still help others.

TRANSFORMED

Looking back, I can see why Professor Kaplan's definition made so much sense to me that day. I realize how those three components—beliefs, actions, and benefits—played out in my life.

I started figuring out what I believed at the age of ten. During those formative years, I attended a local church where I was taught the foundations of the Christian faith. I was always an eager student and loved what I was learning. As the time for baptism came, I pulled back and did not make the commitment. I had so many unanswered questions. For example, even in Sunday school, the general belief was that every human lived in the flesh and could not live up to biblical standards. This made no sense to me, and I asked myself, *How can I commit to something I will never live up to?* My critical thinking said only a hypocrite would do that, and I wasn't going to be one of those. For over a decade, this realization prompted me to veer off in a different direction.

In my midteens, I attended NKST Secondary School Zaki Biam, a school built by Christian missionaries. During this time, I was out

---

14   Genesis 45:5.

to prove that every person who called themselves a Christian was a hypocrite. It's kind of funny now, when I think back on this time. I remember watching kids in my class who considered themselves Christians and then doing whatever I could to discredit them. Sure enough, I witnessed a good amount of hypocrisy. It further reinforced my belief that Christianity was for those who were insincere.

Fast-forward a few years later to 1985, and I had gained admission to study engineering at the University of Port Harcourt, located in the southern part of Nigeria. I arrived several days before the school session started and found myself stranded, as there were no hotels nearby. Fortunately, I met a postgraduate student named Udoh. He accepted me, a stranger, as his guest for the night, and I ended up staying with him for an entire week. Udoh was a Christian, and I quickly discovered that his kindness was deeply rooted in his Christian faith. I remember thinking, *So not all Christians are hypocrites, and they can do good things!*

At Udoh's invitation, and several times, I attended meetings with other Christians on the university campus. Unfortunately, before long, the same issues from my past started to creep up again, and I quickly grew tired of the shortcomings I witnessed among professing believers. I jettisoned the Christian faith for the rest of my years at the university, though I no longer tried to discredit believers.

After graduating, I was sent to Sokoto for a one-year program called the National Youth Service Corps (NYSC).[15] From a geographical perspective, these two cities are at extremes. While Port Harcourt is situated in the southeast region of Nigeria, Sokoto is in the northwest. After one month in orientation camp, I was assigned to Kamba, a border town whose inhabitants, like most others in the

---

15   "National Youth Service Corps," Wikipedia (Wikimedia Foundation, December 9, 2022), https://en.wikipedia.org/wiki/National_Youth_Service_Corps.

state, were predominantly Muslims. Kamba (presently in Kebbi State) is within Nigeria but is positioned at the border with Niger and Benin Republic. I would complete the program by teaching Introductory Technology and Physics at Government Secondary School Kamba.

Jones, a fellow corps member, and I arrived at the school just as they were having a graduation party for some Christian students. Pastor Patrick, who became my close friend, hosted the program. He also taught at the school. A few weeks later, Pastor Patrick invited me to church, but I rudely declined. However, he didn't seem sad or exasperated with my response, and his genuine humility touched me. Moreover, I can still picture him humbly leaving my house that Sunday morning.

Some months later, he invited me again. This time, I accepted and went. I also attended Bible study and other church programs. It was quickly evident to me that Pastor Patrick needed help. All the church programs required some level of literacy to lead, but there weren't many people who could read and write, leaving the pastor to do much of the work himself. One day, he asked me, "Brother Tese, could you please help lead the Bible study?"

"Me? No, Pastor," I responded.

He insisted, promising to help me during the preparation. He was unaware that my problem wasn't a lack of knowledge or inability to teach. No, my real challenge stemmed from what I already knew. I understood what the Bible says about those who teach but do not practice what they preach.

Despite my initial refusal, Pastor Patrick persisted. Eventually, I decided to give it a trial run. I can't remember what I taught during that first Bible study, but it was a short lesson. It was only thirty minutes instead of the usual two hours!

In the end, Pastor Patrick hugged me, saying, "Brother Tese, you are a gifted teacher. From now on, you will be the one leading our Bible study." Other church members made similar comments of appreciation. For some, the shortness of my lesson was likely a more critical factor than its content!

Those responses encouraged me, but I felt very conflicted. I had become the exact hypocrite I had worked hard over the years to discredit—teaching others what I wasn't practicing. As a result, I regretted ever accepting Pastor Patrick's invitation to teach. This battle went on in my heart for several months.

Finally, I had a breakthrough because of God's answer to my prayer. As I grew more involved in the church, one night I had a terrible dream that frightened me about the safety of my family members. Pastor Patrick encouraged me to seek God through a time of prayer and fasting. It was the first time I ever did anything like this. Alas, a few weeks later, I received a letter from my elder sister with news that our elder brother, Tyosue, had an accident. While riding on a motorbike, he collided with a car at a crossroads. The motorbike was damaged beyond repair, but miraculously (and I do not use that word loosely) he survived with a minor scratch on his finger. I knew God had answered my prayer and prevented the imminent disaster that could have befallen my family. That was the day I decided to put my faith in Jesus Christ, ending my years of searching. Since then, I have never looked back.

APPRAISED

In subsequent stages of my formative years, several others also acted on their beliefs for my benefit. One such person was Dominic Ichaba.

The year 1997 was an important one in my personal history. Mhide and I got married earlier that year. There was nothing better than waking up beside the love of my life every morning.

In those days, I worked in an oil and gas services company, where performance evaluations were essential to career progression. We conducted them yearly, and I liked them, as I usually got good scores. So I brought the same appraisal system home—a huge mistake! Two months into our marriage, I asked Mhide to evaluate my role as her husband. Unfortunately, the outcome was remarkably different from my expectation.

From my perspective, things were going well, and I expected a close-to-perfect score. However, Mhide gave me a meager 40 percent. She even pointed out that this was rather generous! It was the worst score in my history of performance appraisals.

As a result, we went to Dominic and Chidi Ichaba for help. They were older than us, with a noticeably wonderful marriage. They graciously accepted and began mentoring us. Fortunately, it didn't take long before I learned that a job appraisal system is an inappropriate tool to measure love!

My challenges with Mhide were not the only ones I faced in 1997. Later that year, they promoted me to supervise a team of about a dozen engineers. Like my marriage, I also started on the wrong foot in this new position. The enormous problem was meeting my manager's and team members' opposing expectations. I expressed my frustrations to Dominic. Using the Bible, he took me through my first structured lesson in leadership.

Dominic used three metaphors to teach me the fundamentals of leadership. He showed me that a leader is a shepherd, servant, and steward. I found this way of looking at leadership extremely helpful.

Since then, I have delved deeper into leadership metaphors. Parts II and III of this book are the results of my findings.

I am genuinely grateful to Dominic and Chidi, who acted on their faith and gave us a firm foundation in both marriage and leadership. It feels like our wedding was yesterday, but Mhide and I have just celebrated twenty-five solid years of happy marriage and are blessed with five lovely kids.

"The key to all action lies in belief," according to an English proverb. Therefore, pause and evaluate your beliefs. Then, consider how you can act on them to create excellent outcomes without imposing unacceptable costs on others. That is the mindset of true leaders.

CHAPTER 2

CONCEPTS

When the rhythm of the drumbeat changes, the dance steps must adapt.
—NAMIBIAN PROVERB

In this chapter, we shall consider key concepts usually linked to leadership, such as followers, influence, and authority. I've taken a critical look at each of them and, in some cases, considered their origins. My findings recorded here are not copied and pasted from popular sources. Instead, I have analyzed them based on present realities, my observations, and my experience. They are a critical foundation for subsequent chapters. Even if you are very familiar with these terms, I encourage you to read my views on them with an open mind.

FOLLOWERS

We have already established that leaders act on their beliefs for the benefit of others. Some of these "others" may end up following the leader. However, not everyone will follow you. Also, you should not expect them to do so, regardless of what you have done for them.

Since ancient times, many great men and women stood up for what was right, but few people (if any) joined them. For example, ancient prophets such as Jeremiah, Ezekiel, and Micaiah[16] were the lone voices of their days. Only from a historical perspective do we value their impact. Can we say these individuals were leaders? I believe they were.

Contrast that with social media platforms today that make it possible to have and even buy countless followers. Take Cristiano Ronaldo, a man with over 455 million followers on Instagram.[17] How many would consider him a great leader? Similarly, celebrities like Tiwa Savage, Bruna Tatiana, Virat Kohli, Naomi Watanabe, Huda Kattan, Anne Curtis, and Andy Lau have many followers. Still, some may find it challenging to think of them as true leaders.

If we look at our social media platforms, not many people follow us because we are leaders. I follow many people, even companies, to keep myself informed of what is happening. I also have followers, but this says nothing about my ability to lead them. To follow, you click. When you want to stop following, you click again. That's all. None of this is about leadership.

Let's consider what happened during Jesus's arrest. Mark reported, *"Then everyone deserted him and fled."*[18] So, does it mean Jesus ceased to be a leader because all the followers abandoned him? Well, of course not.

To sum up, the widespread perception that a leader must have followers is flawed. Indeed, there are leaders with followers, but we cannot generalize and say it must always be that way.

---

16   1 Kings 22.

17   Statista.com, "Instagram Accounts with the Most Followers Worldwide as of June 2022," accessed November 14, 2022, https://www.statista.com/statistics/421169/most-followers-instagram/.

18   Mark 14:50.

INFLUENCE

Influence is a phenomenon many people use nowadays to define leadership. The word "influence" can be traced back to its medieval Latin root, *influentialia*, meaning to flow into, visitation, or outbreak. When an outbreak of a disease called "influenza" or "flu" first occurred, unsure how it came about, the Italians called it *"influenza di stelle,"* meaning influence from the stars. The impact—sickness and death— could be seen and felt, but the cause was superstitious speculation.[19]

Also, Merriam-Webster defines influence as "the power or capacity of causing an effect in indirect or intangible ways."[20] In other words, there is no easy connection between cause and effect regarding *influence.*

If we define leadership as influence, we will need adequate evidence of what we have discovered that those who used the word for the first time did not know. Otherwise, we turn leadership into a mystery. However, leadership is not a mystery. It can be learned, understood, and practiced.

Even when leadership results in influence, we can hardly trace which aspect of leadership caused it. Furthermore, we can't determine in advance what the influence will be. Therefore, it fails to paint an accurate picture when leadership is defined solely as influence.

I remember with gratitude Mr. George Varghese, my secondary school mathematics and physics teacher. He was a generous man and offered his students extra lessons for free. At the end of his contract with the school, he stayed several months without a salary to support us till graduation. Many of us in the class benefited from his sacrifice,

---

19 Wikipedia, "Influenza," last updated October 27, 2022, https://en.wikipedia.org/wiki/Influenza.

20 Merriam-Webster.com, "Influence," accessed February 1, 2022, https://www.merriam-webster.com/dictionary/influence.

yet I'm the only one who eventually followed his career path. Though he didn't choose for me, I could emphasize that Mr. George influenced me. Nevertheless, I remain fully responsible for my decision to study electrical engineering.

In some cases, influence does not even happen in one's lifetime. Take the story of Mohamed Bouazizi. Born in Tunisia, Bouazizi was a street seller who experienced ongoing harassment by the police. On December 17, 2010, he grew so frustrated with the persecution that he covered himself in gasoline and set himself ablaze. An onlooker captured this self-immolation on video and posted it to Facebook. When Bouazizi set himself on fire, few people knew him. However, his action that day sparked the Arab Spring, bringing profound change to the region.[21]

In the United States, on May 25, 2020, people were horrified to witness the death of an African American named George Floyd. While few people knew Floyd before this incident, his murder at the hands of a Minneapolis police officer prompted worldwide protests.[22]

In the 1960s, meteorologist Edward Lorenz discovered that "small changes in initial conditions can lead to large-scale and unpredictable variation in the future state of the system."[23] This discovery is called the "butterfly effect." It is a fitting description of how individuals such as Bouazizi and Floyd have impacted society. Influence functions in the same manner.

If we wake up in the morning with a plan to go and influence someone, most likely we will return home disappointed. We can do

21   Wikipedia, "Mohamed Bouazizi," last updated November 8, 2022, https://en.wikipedia.org/wiki/Mohamed_Bouazizi.

22   Wikipedia, "George Floyd," last updated November 5, 2022, https://en.wikipedia.org/wiki/George_Floyd/.

23   Merriam-Webster.com, "Butterfly Effect," accessed February 1, 2022, https://www.merriam-webster.com/dictionary/butterfly%20effect.

all the right things, but ultimately the decision to change is not in our hands but theirs. Therefore, trying to predict or control influence is an exercise in futility. This understanding helps me curtail unnecessary stress and disappointments when people do not act as I wish.

As I write this book, I pray that it will be helpful to every reader. However, I have no guarantee that it will influence anyone. The results are beyond my control.

AUTHORITY

I define authority as the right or permission to use power. Authority, for me, is like electricity. Without it, many modern appliances cease to function as intended. At this point, here are a few definitions to consider from elementary physics:

- Work is done if an object moves toward the applied force. This is useful work.
- Power is the rate of doing work. It is doing useful work repeatedly.
- Therefore, authority is the permission to do useful work repeatedly.

Authority is critical to functionality. The crowd identified authority as the distinguishing mark of Jesus's teachings. See Matthew 7:28–29:

> When Jesus had finished saying these things, the crowds were amazed at his teaching,[29] because he taught as one who had authority, and not as their teachers of the law.

Much later, when assigning his followers a crucial task, he knew they would need it, so Jesus gave them authority.[24]

It is necessary to point out that even our everyday situations require authority. For instance, when you were a teenager, maybe your parents left the house and asked you to look after your younger siblings. In those few hours that you were in charge, you had authority. If you are an elected representative of your constituency, you oversee their affairs for the period of your mandate. Whether you are a pastor, an elder, or an usher in your church, you have some authority in the house of God.

Throughout history, leaders such as Mahatma Gandhi and Nelson Mandela have acknowledged the need for authority before acting. Contrary to some popular views, these men did not act independently. They acted based on the authority given to them. Gandhi was deeply connected to the Natal Indian Congress, an organization he founded in 1894 to fight racial discrimination. Likewise, Mandela joined the African National Congress in 1943 and cofounded its youth league in 1944. These groups provided each man with the authority needed for him to act.

Even Martin Luther King Jr. didn't act alone. He went to Birmingham with the invitation and under the authority of the Southern Christian Leadership Conference, the organization for which he served as president. He stated this fact very clearly in his famous letter from Birmingham City Jail:

> Several months ago our local affiliate here in Birmingham invited us to be on call to engage in a nonviolent direct-action program if such were deemed necessary. We readily consented, and when the hour came we lived up to our

---

24   Matthew 28:18–20.

promises. So I am here, along with several members of my staff, because we were invited here. I am here because I have basic organizational ties here.[25]

As you can see from these examples, leadership requires authority to be effective. However, authority is not a license to oppress others. Instead, we must use it to do valuable work. As former US president and general Dwight D. Eisenhower stated, "You do not lead by hitting people over the head. That's assault, not leadership." Or as Kenyans say, "To lead is not to run roughshod over people."

Authority is not a blank check, and it always has limits. So we must make sure we know and respect these limits. A helpful illustration is the famous American boxer Mike Tyson. During his youth, Tyson had over 150 street fights in New York in the 1980s.[26] "By the age of twelve Tyson had been arrested by the police countless times."[27] His actions violated the authority. However, all of this changed when he transitioned to being a boxer. At the close of his career, Tyson ended with fifty-eight total fights, fifty wins, and only six losses. Known as one of the most dominant fighters of his era, Tyson mercilessly pounded opponents who dared step their foot into the ring.

On the streets, Tyson's actions constituted assault. Conversely, Tyson's actions were permissible within the roped-off ring, and much of the world paused what they were doing to watch. His actions now had authority. However, when Tyson violated this authority, such as when he bit off a part of Evander Holyfield's ear, he was penalized.

---

25 Letter from Birmingham City Jail by Martin Luther King Jr., https://www.csuchico.edu/iege/_assets/documents/susi-letter-from-birmingham-jail.pdf.

26 Hotboxin' with Mike Tyson Clips, "Mike Tyson Had 150 Street Fights before Becoming Pro in Boxing," YouTube, July 29, 2020, 5:36, https://www.youtube.com/watch?v=gyYUPj5woFY.

27 Frank Oliver, *Tyson: The Concise Biography of Iron Mike* (Self-Published, 2011).

So the question is no longer how to lead without authority. For we now know this is not practical. It is instead how to use the authority we already have to do good repeatedly, irrespective of our position in an organization.

POSITION

As explained in chapter 1, leadership is about acting on your beliefs for the benefit of others. Therefore, it is possible to lead from any position. Unfortunately, there is a misconception that only those at the top of an organization can bring about change. Although many chief executives have done great things, you don't have to be one to make a meaningful contribution.

You can also cause change from within the ranks of your company. For example, these days, we know of the company Intel because of its powerful microprocessor chips. However, it wasn't always that way. Initially, Intel manufactured dynamic random-access memory (DRAM), dominating the market for many years. After stiff competition, Intel changed its core business from manufacturing memory chips to microprocessors. This major shift in Intel's core business did not start from the top but from the midlevel staff.[28]

There is an example of leadership from lower down the organizational ladder. It is the maid to the wife of Naaman, the high-profile Aramean army commander. The Bible says the Aramean king sent Naaman to Samaria at the girl's advice. He returned home, healed of his leprosy just as the girl had said.[29] It seems the girl did nothing more than make a simple suggestion. Please note that the raiders had

---

28 Anthony Smoak, "Andy Grove and Intel's Move from Memory to Microprocessors," AnthonySmoak.com, March 27, 2016, https://anthonysmoak.com/2016/03/27/andy-grove-and-intels-move-from-memory-to-microprocessors/.

29 2 Kings 5:1–19.

forcibly abducted her from her family. Besides, she was their maid, not their family doctor. If things didn't work out, she could have been in trouble. Despite the risk, she acted on her faith in God and informed them of the prophet. Her advice transformed Naaman's life for the better. That is leadership, as per our definition in chapter 1.

In business, nonexecutive board members, who are not part of the organization's management, may also initiate change. Most often, they merely advise the executives. Similarly, the wise counsel of a mentor can change someone's life. That is leadership from the outside. Again, the important thing is not the position.

Therefore, irrespective of your position, you can act on your beliefs and achieve remarkable outcomes. You can be a leader; it's a matter of choice, not position.

MANAGEMENT

Let us now consider the subject of management. It has the "Latin root *manus agere*, and it means to act with one's hands. It follows that managers are people who can give a hand when a job needs doing."[30]

Leadership relates to how we deal with people, whereas management relates to how we deal with things—such as products, systems, and processes. The challenge is to hold both in proper balance. If we go too far on the side of leadership and focus exclusively on people, systems and processes can fall apart. Alternatively, if we devote all our attention to managing things and forget the people behind those things, we end up with a disgruntled workforce.

Early in my career, when I worked as an IT support engineer, I had firsthand experience with this point. I enjoyed fixing computer

---

30   Rolf U. Kramer, *The Future Is Yours* (Winchester, UK: John Hunt Publishing, November 29, 2013).

problems. My supervisor, John Gardner, taught me how to write scripts. For many routine tasks, which usually took hours, using scripts, I could complete them with a single command. That was especially exciting. At the end of my first year in this role, I realized that having the end user satisfied was an equally important aspect of my job. I decided then to make a personal goal to give careful attention to my dealings with the end users while ensuring the quality of my work remained high.

John left the company, and I became his temporary replacement for about three months. During that time, many team members distanced themselves from me. When I inquired, one of them told me he understood the importance I placed on client satisfaction. However, trampling the employees to do so was not a good idea. Apparently, I was doing just that.

A leader needs to use both hands— the *leader* hand and the *manager* hand.

That incident taught me that I must consider the needs of all my stakeholders. I also learned that tasks needed to be done and people needed to be attended to at the same time. Another way of saying this is that a leader needs to use both hands—the *leader* hand and the *manager* hand.

Like most people, you will use your right hand more often if you are right-handed. Similarly, if you are left-handed like me, you usually pick up things with your left hand. In any case, you need both hands in many daily situations, and switching between them happens subconsciously. In the same way, whether you are called a team leader or an operations manager, you will always need both hands. This includes knowing how to lead people and how to manage things. Chris Hardesty wrote:

Leadership and management must go hand in hand. They are not the same thing. But they are necessarily linked and complementary. Any effort to separate the two is likely to cause more problems than it solves.[31]

Moving forward, we will take Chris's point seriously. We will not attempt to separate the two but will keep in mind that leadership and management go hand in hand.

SITUATIONAL LEADERSHIP

Ken Blanchard has made the situational leadership concept famous since the 1960s. The idea is that no single "best" leadership style exists. On the contrary, most successful leaders adapt their leadership style to the prevailing situation.[32] I have found this approach extremely helpful.

Critics of this concept think that we can end up with "endless varieties of leadership" and that the executive "looking for a model to help him is hopelessly lost."[33] As a business executive, I can refute this claim. I do not consider myself to be "hopelessly lost." Instead, this concept gave me a clear understanding of leadership.

It's not that we need thousands of varieties of leadership. Think of shoe sizes, for example. Even if we add up all the different sizes worldwide, the number might come up to a little more than a

---

31   Chris Hardesty, "What Is the Difference between Management and Leadership?," *Wall Street Journal*, March 25, 2011, https://www.wsj.com/articles/what-is-the-difference-between-management-and-leadership?tesla=y.

32   Paul Hersey and Kenneth H. Blanchard, *Management of Organizational Behavior*, 10th ed. (London: Pearson, July 18, 2012).

33   Robert Goffee and Gareth Jones, "Why Should Anyone Be Led by You?," Harvard Business School, September 25, 2000, https://hbswk.hbs.edu/archive/why-should-anyone-be-led-by-you.

hundred.[34] Certainly not thousands or millions. Most stores only carry a limited selection of shoes to serve their customers. Still, despite this limited selection, countless customers frequent these shops every day, and most have little trouble finding a size that fits their needs.

We can find another great example in the medical field. No country would think of having an equal number of doctors as they do patients. Instead, one doctor can serve multiple patients in a day and still care for them effectively. Even Sweden, a country credited with the best public health system, has only a little more than five doctors per one thousand people.[35]

We don't need a unique style for every situation. Rather, we can group situations by their common characteristics and apply the relevant leadership styles. That is what situational leadership is all about.

We should also consider the chameleon. It varies its skin coloration as a camouflage. For ages, chameleons have gotten a bit of a bad rap. So often, we describe someone who is disingenuous and with questionable character as a chameleon. This unnatural association is very unfair to this gentle and harmless arboreal creature. Like the chameleon, adapting your leadership to the prevailing circumstances is very legitimate. Bill George, the author of *Authentic Leadership*, wrote, "Good leaders are able to nuance their styles to the demands of the situation, and to know when and how to deploy different styles."[36]

---

34 Size Charter, "Understanding Shoe Sizing," accessed February 21, 2022, https://www.sizecharter.com/clothing-fit-and-measurement/understanding-shoe-sizing.

35 World Atlas, "Countries with the Most Physicians per Capita," accessed February 21, 2022, https://www.worldatlas.com/articles/countries-with-the-most-physicians-per-capita.html.

36 Bill George, *Authentic Leadership* (New York: Wiley, August 1, 2003).

Success will elude us if the situation changes and we don't adapt our leadership. The Namibians aptly put it this way: "When the rhythm of the drumbeat changes, the dance steps must adapt."

However, adapting to a situation must be done with integrity. Without integrity, adapting is simply manipulating, and that is not situational leadership.

METAPHORS

As mentioned earlier, I became keenly interested in leadership after my encounter with Dominic Ichaba in 1997. Since then, I've read countless books and articles, attended many seminars and workshops, and learned much about leadership, even as I have played different leadership roles. At some point, learning became a problem. I had difficulty remembering what concept to apply whenever I faced a real-life situation. I wondered if there was a way to organize all I had learned in a format I could easily remember. Fortunately, using certain occupations as metaphors solved my problem.

The idea of using metaphors is undoubtedly not new. Since ancient times, many have used metaphors to connect with their audiences. Interestingly, some Bible writers also used some of the occupations of their day as metaphors to illustrate their points. For example, the prophet Jeremiah used the metaphors of a potter[37] and a father[38] to pass spiritual lessons to the nation of Israel. The apostle Paul wrote about the farmer, the athlete, and the soldier to illustrate the Christian life in his second letter to Timothy.[39]

---

37 Jeremiah 18 and 19.

38 Jeremiah 35.

39 2 Timothy 2:3–7.

This is true of Jesus as well. Those who listened to his teachings called him a teacher, and those who saw him growing up called him a carpenter. Those were the trades or roles they identified with him, not metaphors. But Jesus did make use of metaphors. An example would be when he said in John 10:11, "I am the good shepherd. The good shepherd lays down his life for the sheep."

There is no evidence that Jesus was a shepherd, which means his statement was a metaphor. He also clarified what quality or aspect represented his point: "The good shepherd lays down his life for the sheep."

The challenge with metaphors is that we can get entangled in their details and miss our main point. A single book cannot be a training manual for physicians and engineers. I certainly do not want the illustrations or the metaphors to enter the limelight and thwart the purpose of this book.

To guard against this, I follow the example of Jesus and explain what aspects or qualities are of particular interest for each metaphor. For instance, we focus mainly on diagnosis, though physicians offer many other important lessons.

Some may feel that the lessons we draw from their professions are too narrow. Please remember that this is about leadership, not a textbook in any other domain. Please exercise some patience and read to the end. When you do, I am confident this book will help you become more versatile in your ability to lead.

In a nutshell, switching to the appropriate metaphor required by the situation is a critical aspect of versatile leadership.

CHAPTER 3

S-CURVE

Even the loftiest and highest mountain begins on the ground.

—AFRICAN PROVERB

In 2017, they invited me to give a talk at a forum for young entrepreneurs. So I took the time to reflect on my entrepreneurial journey. I wondered what I would have appreciated if someone had told me at the beginning. That led me to the business life cycle. I also call it the S-Curve[40] because of its shape. It is worth noting that the S-Curve concept became popular due to Richard N. Foster's book *Innovation: The Attacker's Advantage.*[41] However, Foster's perspective does not limit how I use the S-Curve.

As I reflected, I realized that many aspects of business and human life cycles are similar. The stages in the human life cycle move from fetus, baby, child, adolescent, to adulthood and conclude with the

---

40 The S-Curve here has nothing to do with reverse curve in civil engineering, line of beauty in arts, sigmoid function in mathematics, or the S-Curve in project management.

41 Richard N. Foster, *Innovation: The Attacker's Advantage* (Summit Books, January 1, 1986).

elderly. Similarly, there is a start and an end with various stages in between for everything in life.

This applies to products, churches, and empires. It may take thousands of years for a nation to decline, but history has taught us that each one that has risen has also fallen. Businesses follow a similar pattern. The stages include preparation, start-up, growth, maturity, and decline (Figure 3.1).

Effective leadership requires understanding where your organization is on the S-Curve. In this chapter, we shall look at the characteristics and challenges of each stage. We shall also consider the transitions between them. Dr. Ichak Adizes, the author of *Managing Corporate Lifecycles*, wrote, "Whenever an organization makes the transition from one life cycle stage to the next, difficulties arise."[42]

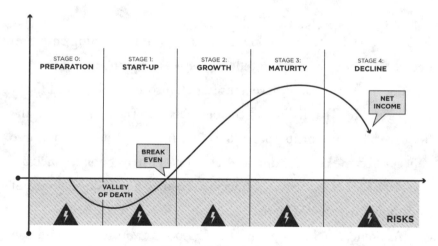

Figure 3.1: The S-Curve

42   Ichak Kalderon Adizes, *Managing Corporate Lifecycles: Complete Edition* (Carpinteria, CA: Adizes Institute Publications, February 2, 2017).

STAGE 0: PREPARATION

The preparation stage is critical but often omitted when describing the business life cycle. It may be the reason many good ideas don't see the light of day. Neeraj Kumar noted this in his viral tweet:

> The best ideas don't die in the marketplace—they die in the shower. People don't give themselves permission to walk out of the shower, write it on a napkin, and take it into the world. They're afraid people will say, "This is just a crazy idea."[43]

Therefore, you should take your idea or dream seriously and plan its implementation.

In our family, like many others, we celebrate birthdays. Everyone knows that there were about nine months of development preceding the birth of each person. Similarly, adequate preparation should happen before a company opens its doors for business. What pregnancy is to human life, preparation is to a venture.

Regardless of how you got into entrepreneurship, please write out your business plan. It will be challenging to convince others that you are serious about your venture if your idea remains in your head.

It is not a big deal if you don't know how to write a business plan. I knew nothing about this process when I decided to establish a company. With very few online sources, I bought books, talked to people, and started writing. Fortunately, these days, countless resources on the internet can serve as a guide for creating a good business plan.

From experience, writing a business plan helps challenge many assumptions, expose faulty concepts, and bring a great dream to life.

---

43   Neeraj Kumar Singal (@nksingal), Twitter post, October 21, 2018, 5:17 a.m., https://twitter.com/nksingal/status/1053938188992069633.

Irrespective of which tools you choose, I strongly recommend that you understand basic finance, especially financial statements. There are three primary financial statements: income statement, balance sheet, and cash flow. Understanding these will help you make a financially viable plan. Setting up a business without knowing your numbers is like playing a game of soccer without keeping the score. How will you know if you are winning or losing?

Take the time to write out the plan yourself. It will be a mistake to pass this responsibility on to someone else. From experience, writing a business plan helps challenge many assumptions, expose faulty concepts, and bring a great dream to life.

The preparation stage ends when you register the venture. Therefore, the registration is akin to a baby being born. A new stage has begun!

STAGE 1: START-UP

Your venture begins activities at the start-up stage. It would be best if you do not start everything at once. Instead, use the minimum viable product (MVP) concept to test and validate your assumptions. MVP differs from industry to industry and company to company. During Google's early days, it focused on doing one thing well: offering the best search engine. There were no Google Maps, Google News, or Gmail. They added these services with time.

Therefore, if you operate a restaurant, you might start with a few items on your menu and expand from there. That is what MVP is all about. The early start-up is a trial-and-error period, and it requires flexibility. It's more than implementing your business plan. It's a matter of being flexible and adaptive to the circumstances. Companies that do *this* well succeed! For example, David Packard, the cofounder of HP, explained what they did during HP's initial period:

> In those early days Bill and I had to be versatile. We had to tackle almost everything ourselves—from inventing and building products to pricing, packaging, and shipping them; from dealing with customers and sales representatives to keeping the books; from writing the ads to sweeping up at the end of the day. Many of the things I learned in this process were invaluable, and not available in business schools.[44]

After those early days, David and Bill changed their style for HP to go past the start-up stage. Some entrepreneurs resist this transition to their detriment.

Great flexibility is needed when a business has to replace its core product. As mentioned in chapter 2, Intel switched from manufacturing DRAM to microprocessors. Nokia was a pulp mill when it started in the nineteenth century but became the worldwide vendor of mobile phones in the late 1990s.[45] These changes were outside their original business plans, but it was just what each company needed to do to remain in business. Generally, a start-up is more likely to alter its core business than a mature company.

The start-up is a difficult stage. The company is new in business, and there is no track record. Getting your first customers on board is a challenging task. We launched Integrated Solutions Angola (ISA), an information technology services company, in 2005. Fortunately, a customer who knew the competence of our founding team members

---

44   David Packard, *The HP Way: How Bill Hewlett and I Built Our Company* (New York: Harper Business, January 3, 2006).

45   Wikipedia, "Nokia," last updated November 5, 2022, https://en.wikipedia.org/wiki/Nokia.

took a chance with us and made cost savings on services. There are other ways also. Some companies offer early adopters free software for a few months. These customers accept to use software that is yet to be thoroughly tested. Thus, creative ways exist to overcome the clients' initial resistance toward start-ups.

Start-ups are generally expensive at the early stage. There is no income, and costs continue to rise. Even when you start making sales, it takes a while before the business reaches a break-even point when its income is just enough to cover its costs. You will have a trough shape if you draw a graph of your net income from when you started spending money during the preparation stage up to the break-even point (see Figure 3.1). Investors call this the "valley of death." It's during this period that start-ups fail the most. If making money is your primary motive, this deadly valley will be an impossible challenge. However, with a more meaningful goal, you will probably cross it.

Despite their technical expertise, some start-ups fail because their managers lack business and leadership skills.

It is difficult to guess how long a company's start-up stage will last. To depart from this stage, a venture must overcome the valley of death, make regular profits, and demonstrate the potential for reliable growth.

STAGE 2: GROWTH

The growth stage brings a time of regular profits combined with more growth opportunities. As desirable as it is, growth has challenges many entrepreneurs often underestimate. Your new hires may not deliver the excellent quality your company is known for, but you don't have the time to train them. You get new orders, but the bank's requirements for a credit line are exacting. Relationships deteriorate as different teams act like rival political parties in an election year. The list goes on. These challenges can undermine growth if you don't address them properly. If the one responsible for the enterprise can't address these issues, replacement may be a reasonable solution.

For example, most people know Steve Jobs as the visionary Apple founder. He was a genius, and his attention to design was unmatched. However, John Sculley made a tremendous contribution to Apple's early growth. Catherine Clifford wrote, "On April 11, 1983, Sculley joined Apple as the CEO. And from 1983 to 1993, he was the CEO. In that time, Apple went from having revenues of $569 million to $8.3 billion."[46] Jobs resigned from the company in 1985 and did not return till 1997. While many rightly attribute Apple's success to Jobs, much of the early growth of Apple happened because of Sculley.

The growth stage also requires setting standards, putting systems in place, and continuously improving them to meet the changing requirements. Depending on your industry, you may adopt an existing standard such as ISO 9001:2015. If appropriately implemented, this quality management system allows your company "to consistently provide products and services that meet customer and applicable statutory and regulatory requirements."[47]

STAGE 3: MATURITY

Stability is a mark of maturity in so many ways. Everyone has come to terms with the expected standard of behavior, and they work together

---

46   Catherine Clifford, "Former Apple CEO John Sculley: What I Learned from Steve Jobs," CNBC, May 29, 2018, https://www.cnbc.com/2018/05/29/what-ex-apple-pepsi-ceo-john-sculley-learned-from-steve-jobs.html.

47   International Organization for Standardization, "ISO 9001:2015(en): Quality Management Systems—Requirements," accessed November 14, 2022, https://www.iso.org/obp/ui/#iso:std:iso:9001:ed-5:v1:en.

in synergy. The brand is known, and profits are predictable. The systems put in place in earlier stages become stable as the company matures. One example is the Toyota Production System (TPS).

Through continuous improvement, Toyota spent decades developing its management system. According to Toyota's website, TPS is "a production system based on the philosophy of achieving the complete elimination of all waste in pursuit of the most efficient methods."[48] I like TPS because of its twin pillars, "just-in-time" and "in-station quality." "Just-in-time" ensures that each process in the chain produces only what the next process requires. Many company cultures punish people for bringing out bad news. In Toyota, the "in-station quality" empowers employees to detect and deal with defects in their stations. No wonder TPS became the precursor to lean management, which nearly all industries now use.[49]

Another distinguishing factor of a mature business is its leaders. Supposing a company is around for fifty years, if the founder is required to show up at work daily, it's not mature yet. Also, if a company loses key staff and struggles, it isn't mature even if it has been in business for a century. A mature business does not require the presence of any particular person to operate effectively. It has a proper mechanism for the succession of its key people. Anyone can quit or retire, yet the company will continue to thrive. When Bill Gates left Microsoft, the company continued to grow under new leadership. Apple became the most valuable company in the world after Steve Jobs died. That's how I measure a mature business.

Some founders mistakenly enjoy the feeling of being indispensable. They love the sense of dependency everyone has on them,

---

48   Toyota, "Toyota Production System," accessed November 14, 2022, https://global. toyota/en/company/vision-and-philosophy/production-system/.

49   Jeffrey K. Liker, *The Toyota Way: 14 Management Principles from the World's Greatest Manufacturer, 2nd ed.* (New York: McGraw Hill, January 7, 2004).

especially since they have been responsible for taking their company through a reasonable period of growth. Please note that serious clients do not trust service providers who depend on specific individuals. Similarly, investors won't fully buy in if your company has been in business for many years but is unstable.

This was something I realized was a problem in my business, and I've been working toward less dependence on myself for several years. I wanted a company where I could take a sabbatical leave and eventually retire without fearing it would collapse or stagnate in my absence. We've made much progress, but ISA is still not 100 percent there yet.

A mature company may have a reasonable period of prosperity with its well-known brand, even without the founder. As time goes on, its leaders may forget its essence. As a result, complacency gives birth to inaction, and arrogance breeds mistakes. Either spoiled child destroys the corporation no matter how long it has existed.

STAGE 4: DECLINE

On the S-Curve, the decline comes after maturity. Realistically, a company can nose-dive from any of the preceding stages. When you realize your company is in a downward spiral, your survival instinct may tell you to press the panic button and stop it quickly. However, the more appropriate objective should be to get out of decline quickly and safely. Yes, safety is critical.

Consider the boys trapped in a cave in Chiang Rai province in northern Thailand. On June 23, 2018, after a practice session, twelve members of a local football team and their assistant coach entered the Tham Luang Nang Non cave. Unfortunately, they were trapped there due to a flood caused by heavy rainfall. Several experts from different countries carefully planned and successfully executed the special rescue operation. It took nine days before divers were able to contact the boys. Though everyone was eager to get them out, it took another week before the first of the boys was rescued. Three days later, all of them were taken out safely. Overall, some of them had spent seventeen days in the flooded cave![50]

Similarly, your company's transition into decline may happen without notice, and you may be racing against time like the trapped boys. However, frantic moves are likely to cause more problems. Taking an organization out of decline is also a risky rescue operation that must be done with utmost care.

Let's now look at some factors that may cause a company to decline. The competition comes up with cheaper products. Market conditions change. Or there is a leadership turnover. Companies are highly vulnerable to decline in a volatile world marked by uncertainties and complexities. As happened to Netflix, a wrong decision by its leaders can make any business tumble. Netflix was formed in 1997 and grew steadily for fourteen years. In 2011, Netflix decided to raise the price of its DVD subscription. Within a quarter, it lost over eight hundred thousand customers, representing about 3 percent of its total subscriptions. However, its stock price plummeted by 77 percent! Fortunately, Netflix recovered from this decline by correcting its mistakes. The introduction of "Netflix Original" also helped its upturn.[51]

Irrespective of the cause, the main signs of decline are the reduction in revenue and profit margins. Small and medium-sized companies can easily become insolvent due to decline. Large companies may afford to live in decline for some time, but if the ship is not righted,

---

50   Matt Gutman, *The Boys in the Cave: Deep Inside the Impossible Rescue in Thailand* (New York, NY: William Morrow, 2018).

51   Sara Green, *Netflix* (Hopkins, MN: Bellwether Media, August 1, 2017).

all will sink. For example, Kodak lived in decline for many years but eventually filed for bankruptcy on January 19, 2012.[52]

Like the boys, it is possible to take a "trapped" company out of decline safely. IBM declined for several years and eventually, in 1993, posted a USD $8 billion loss—at the time, the biggest in American corporate history.[53] However, that wasn't the end for the multinational technology corporation. IBM's recovery from the near-death experience is called corporate turnaround. It is like a start-up overcoming the valley of death and going on to the growth stage. The only difference is that the company is no longer new.

Discussion on the decline stage is incomplete without examining corruption. Corruption destroys institutions and nations. Let us consider the airline industry in Africa. I look back to when I began my international travel in the midnineties. During the first decade, I had used the following African airlines: Nigeria Airways, Air Gabon, Air Afrique, Ethiopian Airways, Kenya Airways, and South African Airways. Here are their statuses as of the time of writing. Ethiopian Airways is the only one still operating profitably. Unfortunately, the good news stops there. South African Airways went bankrupt in 2020. It is undergoing recapitalization in an attempt to bring about its turnaround. Kenya Airways has not made a profit for a decade. Yet there is still more bad news.

Nigeria Airways, Air Gabon, and Air Afrique have gone extinct. Please note that these airlines were not start-ups when they failed. No, they started operations in the 1950s and early 1960s and operated for several decades before they went bankrupt. Each had provided jobs to thousands of people. It is not clear what caused Air Gabon to

---

52 Wikipedia, "Kodak," last updated October 23, 2022, https://en.wikipedia.org/wiki/Kodak.

53 Wikipedia, "IBM," last updated November 14, 2022, https://en.wikipedia.org/wiki/IBM.

fail. However, corruption and mismanagement brought down Nigeria Airways and Air Afrique.[54]

According to International Criminal Police Organization (Interpol):

> The effects of corruption are far-reaching: it can undermine political, social, and economic stability, and ultimately threaten the safety and security of society as a whole.[55]

Corruption thus threatens the entire society! However, each leader must take personal responsibility. I remember one incident that illustrates my point. I was visiting the US and was in a taxi in New York City. The taxi driver happened to be an African like me. Our discussion quickly drifted to corruption in Africa and its impact on the continent. When we arrived at the destination, he asked if he could write a higher amount on the receipt after I had paid him. I wondered why he would do that. He told me that, as individuals, we couldn't change anything and that I should try and help myself. I asked him, "How is this different from what we have just complained about?"

We shouldn't diminish the impact an individual can make. This whole thing is like democracy—every single vote counts. A vote for corruption is a vote for destruction. A clear conscience is priceless, even if you may not change the system.

In conclusion, the S-Curve shows organizations' stages: preparation, start-up, growth, maturity, and decline. The metaphors in parts II and III are helpful to leaders as they navigate the challenges of the S-Curve stages and their transitions.

---

54 Wikipedia, "Nigeria Airways," last updated August 27, 2022, https://en.wikipedia.org/wiki/Nigeria_Airways; Wikipedia, "Air Afrique," last updated July 21, 2022, https://en.wikipedia.org/wiki/Air_Afrique.

55 Interpol, "Corruption," accessed November 14, 2022, https://www.interpol.int/Crimes/Corruption.

PART II

STRATEGY

CHAPTER 4

PHYSICIAN

He who conceals his disease cannot expect to be cured.

—AFRICAN PROVERB

Please remember the definitions and concepts in the previous section—they are the foundation. This section (part II) examines the strategy metaphors. You neither need them for urgent tasks nor actively use them daily. Yet they have far-reaching implications. Fortunately, strategy is not always a complex subject. For instance, General Electric's former chief executive officer Jack Welch wrote:

> "In real life, strategy is actually very straightforward. You pick a general direction and implement like hell."[56]

However, you need to know your organization's actual status to choose a general direction for it. That is what the physician metaphor does. It gives you an insight into how well your company is doing. You can use it for diagnosis when starting a new leadership position, making a periodic evaluation, or preparing a response to a major event.

---

56 Jack Welch, *Winning: The Ultimate Business How-To Book* (New York: Harper Collins, October 13, 2009).

DIAGNOSIS

It's often said that "prescription without diagnosis is malpractice." Good doctors will always start with a diagnosis. They will not begin treatment just because you have pain.

I should point out that I have no medical training. I rarely visit the hospital, and when I do, it is mainly for routine checkups, but 2018 was different. That year, I had three surgeries in one month. On April 11, my wife rushed me to the emergency room for what we later discovered to be the perforation of the duodenum! I was in great pain, yet the doctors carried out several examinations to find out the cause of the pain before they started treatment.

When leaders find themselves in a new situation, they must do what doctors do—make a diagnosis to know the real status of the organization.

One of these examinations was particularly intriguing. It was called endoscopy. It is done with something that looks like a selfie stick, which they call an endoscope. Rather than clipping this onto an iPhone, this flexible rod has a tiny camera embedded in its tip. The doctor pushed it down my throat to my stomach while taking photos of my internal scenery like an enthusiastic tourist. This, among other tests, revealed the perforation of my duodenum.

The more I thought about it, the more I realized this was a great lesson in leadership. When leaders find themselves in a new situation, they must do what doctors do—make a diagnosis to know the real status of the organization. Then, they must analyze and make sense of the information gathered during the diagnosis before they can lead effectively.

My experience in my first management position, as I mentioned in chapter 1, is worth revisiting. As stated, I felt stuck between my boss and my team. What caused my frustration? I desired to see instant change. For this reason, I wasted no time when they put me in charge. I outlined my plans, and I went into action. There was much I did not know. Even the difficult financial situation of the company made no sense to me.

If I had taken the time to study and understand what was going on, my course of action would have been very different. I wouldn't have made any of those proposals that my manager rejected. This highlights the importance of proper diagnosis before taking any significant action.

Furthermore, doctors check the patient's vital signs as a critical first step. Vital signs are "your heart rate, blood pressure, breathing rate, and temperature. These four signs show how well your body is working."[57]

Similarly, a leader must know the vital signs of their organization. In business, we use key performance indicators (KPIs). All leaders must be familiar with their organization's vital signs. At ISA, we have monthly "goal check" meetings to analyze the company's overall health. During this meeting, every manager reports on the progress they have made on their departmental goals. KPIs help us know when we are running out of cash and how well we are doing with our projects. They show the health status of our company.

With the physician metaphor in mind, one of the helpful tools that my company uses yearly is the SWOT analysis. SWOT is an acronym that stands for strengths, weaknesses, opportunities, and threats. Strengths and weaknesses are internal, while opportunities and threats analyze the company's external factors. The outcome of this analysis forms part of our strategic plan for the coming year.

---

57   Plain Language Medical Dictionary, application by the University of Michigan Library, https://apps.lib.umich.edu/medical-dictionary.

Before you make your strategic plans as a leader, you ought to analyze the internal and external factors affecting your organization.

ASSESSMENT

Great physicians do not rely on the diagnosis of others. They make their own assessment. I gained this perspective just before my third surgery in 2018. This operation took place at a different hospital from the first two. Before transferring me to this new hospital, they performed several tests and included the results as supporting documents in the medical report. When I arrived at the new hospital, Dr. Francis Quayson ordered new tests before he started treatment. One lesson I picked up from this interaction was that a leader shouldn't act solely based on the diagnoses of others. Just like Dr. Francis, they must make their own assessment. I recall an experience during my earlier years in management when I served as a temporary location manager. In his handover report, the outgoing manager recommended that two junior staff be laid off. However, I chose to work with Terry and Charlie to assess them myself. Terry was a terrific guy who did his job well. I couldn't find any basis to act against him, so he remained employed. Charlie, on the other hand, had serious issues, and I eventually let him go.

Leaders must make their own assessments. That is what Saint Luke, a physician, did when he wrote about the life of Jesus. He didn't just write based on what Mark and Matthew wrote. Though these were reliable sources, Dr. Luke did his own investigation. He said:

> Many have undertaken to draw up an account of the things that have been fulfilled among us … With this in mind, since I myself have carefully investigated everything

from the beginning, I too decided to write an orderly account for you, most excellent Theophilus.[58]

Before he wrote, Luke investigated. Similarly, do your assessment before you write out your strategic plans.

Thus, when entering a new situation or facing a major event, use the physician metaphor to diagnose properly before deciding on a strategic course of action.

PANDEMIC AND OVERDOSE

Sometimes, a major event will also necessitate using the physician metaphor for a proper assessment before a strategic response. For example, on March 11, 2020, the World Health Organization declared COVID-19 a pandemic. On its second anniversary, COVID-19 had cumulatively caused over 455 million infections, of which over 6 million people had died.[59] At the onset, there were evacuations. Then the lockdowns brought everything to a standstill. Where should a leader start his response to such a major event? I believe that the physician metaphor is a good starting point. It helps you to carefully assess the situation so that your response can be appropriate.

At ISA, we assessed everything at the onset of the COVID-19 pandemic. We looked at what we needed for everyone to stay safe based on the available information. We also considered ways to keep our company operating when the lockdowns eventually started. We rehearsed our plans and had everything fine-tuned a day before the Angolan government announced the first COVID-19 lockdown

---

58   Luke 1:1–3.

59   "Coronavirus Disease (Covid-19) Pandemic," who.int (World Health Organization), accessed January 26, 2023, https://www.who.int/europe/emergencies/situations/covid-19.

on March 20, 2020. The outcome was that we operated optimally through the many lockdowns.

We started our ISO9001:2015 certification project during the first week of the first lockdown. Fortunately, we completed the project on time and within budget, and the average performance of our staff was at an all-time high. The commitment of our people to implement what we agreed on was crucial to this achievement. Equally important was the diagnosis we did at the beginning. That is one of the reasons I recommend that leaders use the physician metaphor to make an assessment when an event requires a strategic response.

When responding to a major event, we can also learn from good physicians who carefully prescribe the right amount of medication. In doing so, they ensure their patients do not join the ranks of 150,000 people who die yearly from overdoses.[60] The threat of overdose exists in leadership as well as medicine. For example, Russia invaded Ukraine on February 24, 2022. They bombed numerous cities and killed thousands of people, including women and children. After the first seven months of the war, "The Office of the United Nations High Commissioner for Refugees (UNHCR) has estimated that more than 8.7 million people have fled Ukraine and more than 8 million Ukrainians are internally displaced. This is the fastest forced population movement since the Second World War."[61]

What led to this war? Ukraine's attempt to join the North Atlantic Treaty Organization (NATO) was a red line for Russia's president, Vladimir Putin.[62] There's evidence that Russia's leadership

---

60   World Health Organization, "Opioid Overdose," accessed November 14, 2022, https://www.who.int/news-room/fact-sheets/detail/opioid-overdose.

61   United Nations, "The UN and the War in Ukraine: Key Information," September 3, 2022, https://unric.org/en/the-un-and-the-war-in-ukraine-key-information/.

62   Wikipedia, "Russo-Ukrainian War," last updated November 14, 2022, https://en.wikipedia.org/wiki/Russo-Ukrainian_War#2021%E2%80%932022_Russian_military_buildup.

did not make an impulsive decision but took time to think about the situation before starting the war.[63] However, no matter what the Russians diagnosed as the problem, full-scale war is undoubtedly an overdose—and quite literally overkill. Said differently, "The cure is worse than the disease."

Thus, when a leader gets into a new situation or is faced with a major event, the physician metaphor will help them diagnose. Depending on what they find out, the remaining chapters in part II will provide the metaphors for a fitting strategic response.

---

63   Paul Kirby, "Ukraine Conflict: Who's in Putin's Inner Circle and Running the War?," BBCNews.com, March 3, 2022, https://www.bbc.com/news/world-europe-60573261.

CHAPTER 5

ARCHITECT

The eye crosses the river before the body.
—AFRICAN PROVERB

When starting anything new, such as a company, division, department, or movement, use the architect metaphor to articulate your vision. This metaphor is also valuable for developing a realistic plan to bring that vision to reality.

IN STUDIO

In 2006, we purchased one residential property in Luanda. When I visited his office, the developer showed me a brochure with a detailed layout of a condominium. The photos resembled a finished project of sixteen beautiful semidetached houses. Shortly after we spoke, we visited the site, but it was an empty area. Other than the anthills, there was no structure on the ground. Yet interestingly, two years later, it all looked like what he showed me initially.

Architects teach us how to translate a dream or an idea into something definite. What they do in the studio is like what leaders should do during the S-Curve preparation stage, covered in chapter 3. In the studio, an architect sketches out what seems to the owner like a finished project. Then, they make detailed drawings for different teams involved in the construction—electrical wiring drawings for the electricians and plumbing diagrams for the plumbers. Each category only needs to know the aspect of its role in the project in order to carry out its work effectively. In the same way, during the preparation stage, a leader needs to create a strategic vision for the organization. Then, they should develop a detailed business plan with sections that different teams or departments can implement.

In addition, like the architect, you must be there to oversee the implementation process.

ON-SITE

Architects know that magnificent building results from a superb design built according to plan. For this reason, architects make site visits to oversee the construction. They call this "construction administration." The leader using the architect metaphor should likewise supervise the implementation of the strategic plans, especially at the start-up stage.

King Pharaoh of Egypt seemed to have understood this concept. He had a dream, and Joseph correctly interpreted it. Like an architect, Joseph outlined an excellent plan that would diminish the impact of the looming economic crisis if implemented. The Bible says, "The plan seemed good to Pharaoh and to all his officials … Then Pharaoh said to Joseph, 'I hereby put you in charge of the whole land of Egypt.'"[64]

What Pharoah did makes perfect sense because plans could change or take a more distinct form during implementation. Sometimes, materials that come with the building plan are substituted due to

---

64   Genesis 41:37–41.

availability, price, or technology changes. In such situations, the architect will be there to make decisions quickly.

In the business world, companies like HP and Sony Corporation started without a clear vision. Yet Jim Collins still considers them visionary companies because they have grown, lasted long, and made a global impact.[65]

Let me borrow a term from Chris McGoff to explain what Sony and HP did. Their visions were "dynamically incomplete" initially. Chris wrote:

> People develop a sense of ownership in what they help to create … Having members of the group own the vision makes it more likely to succeed. *Dynamic incompleteness* adheres to the truth that too much form causes resistance, and too much void causes chaos. The leader's job is to bring just enough form to inspire the people and frame what needs to be articulated. In a nutshell, that is the art of visioning.[66]

Leaders must have a lot of openness and flexibility to engage in such an open vision process. However, with the uncertainties and complexities in the world, the chances of success are higher with cocreated visions.

Realizing this, we changed our strategic planning process. First, we start with a detailed current corporate profile with sections such as core values, financial statements, clients, products,

With the uncertainties and complexities in the world, the chances of success are higher with cocreated visions.

---

65   Jim Collins and Jerry I. Porras, *Built to Last* (New York: HarperCollins, October 26, 1994).

66   Chris McGoff, *The Primes: How Any Group Can Solve Any Problem* (New York: Wiley, 2012).

and services. Second, we change the date on the profile document to a later date (such as five years from now). Third, we update the profile based on what we anticipate the company will look like at this future date. Fourth, we use scenario planning to create flexible goals and strategies linked to the different scenarios.

Please note that war games (military scenario planning) have been around for centuries. Shell brought it into its management processes in the 1970s. Since then, its use has extended to different kinds of groups.[67]

Based on my understanding, I define scenario planning as a method of making flexible plans with different perspectives of what could happen in the future. We have integrated it into our strategic planning framework for several years. I recommend that leaders in uncertain situations integrate scenario planning into their strategic planning processes.

There are many other ways to go about defining a vision. Whichever approach you choose, ensure it gets implemented so that you don't end up with an abandoned project.

ELEPHANTS AND TOWERS

When you travel around Africa, you will see many abandoned projects, but one of them is inconceivable. It is the Ajaokuta Steel Mill in Nigeria. This is a gigantic project covering an area of twenty-four thousand hectares. After more than a decade of preparation, it started in 1979. It is considered a city on its own. In the late 1980s, I worked there for three months as a student in an industrial training program. Unfortunately, more than forty years after its launch, the colossal

---

67   Paul Schoemaker, *Profiting from Uncertainty: Strategies for Succeeding No Matter What the Future Brings* (New York: Free Press, 2002).

project remains unfinished.[68] It is a failed project in the category called "white elephant." It is immense but doesn't materialize, just like a white elephant. Within your organization, you must avoid such grandiose and unfeasible projects.

In 1997, Taisei Corporation of Japan designed a futuristic skyscraper called the X-Seed 4000. It represents a comical illustration of such an ambitious but fruitless undertaking. The four-kilometer-tall superstructure is nearly five times as tall as Burj Khalifa (the world's tallest building as of 2022). They estimated its construction cost at an outrageous USD $1 trillion! Its proposed site is the Pacific Ring of Fire, the most active volcanic area on earth. The megatower would actively protect its residents from any such disturbances. As expected, the superstructure for a million inhabitants was not for construction! Instead, "the purpose of the plan was to earn some recognition for the firm, and it worked."[69]

Leaders should avoid white elephant visions like the X-Seed 4000 and Ajaokuta Steel Mill. They need to focus resources on what they could build to completion with tangible benefits.

This takes us to another architectural landmark, the Tower of Pisa—Italy's largest tourist attraction. It was designed to be a perfect, vertical sixty-meter structure, but it leaned severely over time. As a result, major remedial work had to be done several times to straighten the structure to about a four-degree angle. This twelfth-century architectural failure has become a famous tourist attraction![70]

---

68   Wikipedia, "Ajaokuta Steel Mill," last updated October 1, 2022, https://en.wikipedia.org/wiki/Ajaokuta_Steel_Mill.

69   Wikipedia, "X-Seed 4000," last updated November 11, 2022, https://en.wikipedia.org/wiki/X-Seed_4000.

70   Charles River Editors, *The Leaning Tower of Pisa: The History and Legacy of Italy's Most Unique Building* (California: CreateSpace Independent Publishing Platform, August 15, 2017).

Leaders should avoid such mistakes by taking to heart the words of Australian architect Harry Seidler: "Architecture is not an inspirational business, it's a rational procedure to do sensible and hopefully beautiful things; that's all."[71] Indeed, sensible outcomes should be the focus of leaders as well.

That doesn't mean that visions are always easy to accomplish. On the contrary, many leaders whose lives embody the architect metaphor had to deal with complex challenges that stood in their way. As a result, some didn't even see the vision materialize during their lifetime.

VISIONARIES

Consider the biblical leader Moses to whom God gave the vision of establishing Israel as a nation. Unfortunately, they were slaves in Egypt, a powerful kingdom of that era. The king of Egypt wasn't willing to let go of the cheap labor that had become engrained in the fabric of his society. This reluctance resulted in devastating consequences for Egypt. Finally, the king chased them out of his country after a terrible personal loss. Just as the Tiv people of central Nigeria say, "A borrowed shirt must be returned to the owner, no matter how much it fits you."

While in the wilderness, Moses carefully mapped out Canaan, the land of destiny for the liberated people. Though he never entered it, Moses wrote out the laws that would govern their conduct. These laws are still in use to this day.

Modern-day Singapore transitioned from a third-world country to a first-world country within forty years under the visionary leader-

---

71   Joseph Demakis, *The Ultimate Book of Quotations* (California: CreateSpace Independent Publishing Platform, November 19, 2012).

ship of Lee Kuan Yew. Bill Gates built a business empire with the vision of "a computer on every desk and in every home."[72]

Kwame Nkrumah, the visionary Ghanaian president and an advocate of Pan-Africanism, painted a detailed vision of a united Africa in 1963 at the first summit of the Organization of African Unity. He said (quoted in part):

> "Your Excellencies, with these steps, I submit, we shall be irrevocably committed to the road which will bring us to a Union Government of Africa."[73]

Nkrumah had properly envisioned much of what we know today as African Union.

So be the architect if you are starting anything new, such as a product, company, family, church, nation, or movement. The architect metaphor will help you sketch a clear vision and a practical blueprint for your organization.

---

72   Daniel Smith, *How to Think Like Bill Gates* (London: Michael O'Mara, October 1, 2016).

73   Lawrence Lupalo, *Three African Visionaries: Nkrumah Nyerere Senghor* (California: CreateSpace Independent Publishing Platform, February 2, 2019).

CHAPTER 6

BUILDER

A house built with wise counsel is not easily shaken.
—ANGOLAN PROVERB

Once you have diagnosed a leadership situation using the physician metaphor and discovered that the organization is healthy and with a clear vision, be careful not to discard the existing systems and processes quickly. Instead, use the builder metaphor to understand and execute the vision and achieve great success.

John Sculley did the same thing when he joined Apple. Instead of developing a new vision for the firm, he focused on growth, implementing Steve Jobs's vision. So it's not surprising that Apple's first golden age occurred during Sculley's leadership. By the tenth year as CEO, Apple's annual income was more than tenfold as it was when he joined.[74] He successfully transitioned Apple from start-up to growth stage.

There is much to be learned from leaders who are builders. They are the ones that can transform start-ups into thriving companies.

---

74 Wikipedia, "John Sculley," last updated November 11, 2022, https://en.wikipedia.org/wiki/John_Sculley.

GROUNDWORK

Before laying the first block, a building contractor must understand the architectural plan and specifications. Builders usually start from the ground up once they know the blueprint. More than anything else, the foundation determines the strength and stability of the structure. Jesus taught that the way we lay the foundation will show how wise or foolish we are.[75] No organization can exist without people. Therefore, they are the foundation. You should value them if you are serious about transitioning your organization into growth and sustainability.

In the construction sector, the living and working conditions of workers are often substandard. Yet since ancient times, these low-income workers have built everything. They are true heroes. Without them, none of the iconic buildings, such as the Taj Mahal, Great Pyramid of Giza, Eiffel Tower, Museo Soumaya, Dominican Chapel, Great Mosque of Djenné, and Sydney Opera House, would exist. It means that leaders must treat them with dignity and respect.

In the technology industry, we do a lot to attract talented individuals and do even more to keep them. Yet from time to time, some would leave. I have noticed tensions rise at the point of departure and relationships turn sour. It is a sensitive period that leaders must handle with great care using the diplomat metaphor discussed in chapter 15. At ISA, we seek to maintain a long-term relationship with our ex-colleagues. We consider them our ambassadors and do everything necessary to help them succeed in their new endeavors, regardless of the reasons and circumstances of their departure.

People are the foundation. As a leader, you need the right people inside and outside for your organization to keep thriving well into the future.

---

75   Matthew 7:24–27.

BUILD TO LAST

Like a house, an organization must be built with quality for it to last. Sadly, this is not always the case. Statistics show that "an average of 8 building collapse disasters occur every year worldwide, resulting in 343 deaths/year. Each event kills an average of 38 persons."[76] Benjamin Franklin said, "The bitterness of poor quality remains long after the sweetness of low price is forgotten." Poor quality is dangerous both in construction and in leadership.

Another worrying set of statistics is that 96 percent of businesses fail worldwide before their tenth anniversary. However, the life expectancy of enterprises should not be that short. Standard Bank of South Africa has been operating since 1862, while HarperCollins Publishers started in the US in 1817. Sennen No Yu Koman Hotel in Japan holds the record as one of the oldest businesses in the world and has been operating continuously since AD 717. By comparison, the tenth-anniversary casualties for businesses are akin to infant mortality. There are "ways to beat the odds and not strengthen the statistics," wrote Jurie Van Dyk.[77]

The builder metaphor can help you beat the odds and build your business to last a long time, serving many generations.

As I write this, ISA is still in its "teens," and we are still building the company. However, I foresee it joining the ranks of centennial companies celebrating their hundredth anniversary. I will no longer be in charge, and most likely my sojourn on earth will have been over, but I foresee the elaborate celebration taking place and someone reading this chapter at that event.

---

76   Mark Keim, "When Buildings Collapse," DisasterDoc.org, June 28, 2021, https://disasterdoc.org/when-buildings-collapse/.

77   Jurie Van Dyk, "Why 9 out of 10 Small Businesses Fail," CreativeOverflow.net, April 12, 2010, http://creativeoverflow.net/why-9-out-of-10-small-businesses-fail/.

To build something that will last also means you must build with quality. Those in the construction industry know that quality is in the details. For this reason, architectural drawings come with detailed plans and specifications. Architect Dennis Kyeyune, the owner of Design Garage Studio, a Ugandan architectural firm, said that many architects even specify how the paint is to be applied.[78]

Despite all these measures, builders still have plenty of room to determine the quality of what they build. If they are not committed to quality, the finished product will be inferior, regardless of the architect's and structural engineer's specifications.

In the same way, those who want to use the builder metaphor to grow their business must be committed to quality. Otherwise, they are building sandcastles that will not last. That's why Apostle Paul said in 1 Corinthians 3:12–14:

> If anyone builds on this foundation using gold, silver, costly stones, wood, hay or straw, their work will be shown for what it is because the Day will bring it to light. It will be revealed with fire, and the fire will test the quality of each person's work. If what has been built survives, the builder will receive a reward.

If you want your organization to stand any stress test, continue to thrive, and make an excellent contribution for centuries, then build with quality. Build it to last. That is what great builders do.

Just because you start with a plan made by someone else doesn't mean the builder's job is easy. Consider Joshua, who took over the leadership of Israel after Moses died. Moses gave a detailed blueprint on one side of the River Jordan, but the Promised Land was on the other. Implementing Moses's plan required crossing over into ter-

---

78   Dennis Kyeyune, personal communication, March 15, 2022.

ritories that were not empty and were heavily fortified, like the city of Jericho.

To be successful, Joshua was admonished several times to be strong and courageous.[79] These qualities are necessary for challenging duties. You don't have to be strong to deal with the easy stuff. Simple errands don't require courage either. Therefore, implementing an existing vision can also be an arduous task.

Apart from strength and courage, a builder also needs wisdom. On the surface, Solomon's job looked straightforward. He took over the leadership of the kingdom of Israel when the wars that had bogged down most of his father's reign had ended. His father, David, left him a clear plan and funds for constructing the temple. Yet he knew that he needed wisdom to be successful. For this reason, Solomon asked for wisdom and nothing else when he had the opportunity.[80]

No wonder the Ovimbundu people of Angola say, "A house built with wise counsel is not easily shaken." Let us, therefore, build our organizations with discernment, so they stand the test of time. Build them to last.

RECOGNITION

I have visited Burj Khalifa many times. It still holds the record as the tallest building in the world.[81] Thousands of individuals representing several companies contributed to making this project a reality. The project's historical records show that an individual, Adrian Smith, was the chief architect and a company (Samsung C&T) was the main builder. So why treat architects and builders differently?

---

79   Joshua 1:6, 7, 9, 18.

80   2 Chronicles 1:7–12.

81   Guinness World Records, "Tallest Building," accessed November 14, 2022, https://www.guinnessworldrecords.com/world-records/tallest-building.

These days, architects work in teams, especially for complex projects. However, a single architect can design something on his own that works but not so with builders. One person alone can't build anything that can serve any meaningful purpose. Therefore, teamwork is more than a buzzword for builders. For example, "More than 12,000 people worked on-site at any given time during the building of Burj Khalifa."[82] Therefore, it would take a great deal of work to recognize each individual builder.

Unfortunately, the lack of recognition for leaders who are builders frustrates some elected public officeholders. "Why should I commit more funds to a past governor's project that I defeated in the last election?" they ask. This is one of the reasons why Nigeria has fifty-six thousand abandoned public projects worth an estimated USD $24 billion.[83] The one who gets the credit is the one who started the project. Thus, completing a project started by others leaves the public office holder with nothing for their legacy.

Organizations are built when people work, not when they scramble for credit. Getting the job done should be your primary focus as a leader.

There are two ways a leader can solve this problem. First, they need to consider the advice of Indira Gandhi. Indira was also a public elected officeholder, yet she said, "There are two kinds of people, those who do the work and those who take the credit. Try to be in the first group; there is less competition there."[84]

---

82 "The Inspiring Story Behind the World's Tallest Tower," https://www.burjkhalifa.ae/en/ (Burj Khalifa), accessed January 26, 2023, https://www.burjkhalifa.ae/en/the-stories.aspx#:~:text=More%20than%2012%2C000%20people%20worked,Work%2D Action%2DResolution).

83 Vanguard, "Nigeria's 56,000 Abandoned Projects," December 21, 2021, https://www.vanguardngr.com/2021/12/nigerias-56000-abandoned-projects/.

84 Sandy Foster, *Say What?* (lulu.com, January 21, 2011).

Organizations are built when people work, not when they scramble for credit. Getting the job done should be your primary focus as a leader.

Second, with so many abandoned projects, it is a niche market on its own, a great opportunity. You will be a hero and become known as the one who revived abandoned projects and brought them to completion. It's a market that doesn't yet have competition. Our world is in desperate need of leaders who are builders.

CHAPTER 7

ENGINEER

That which gains the attention of a leader will be solved.
—UGANDAN PROVERB

As an engineer, I must remind myself that this is not an engineering training manual. Instead, it is about learning from engineers how to solve significant problems that organizations face.

Engineers solve problems and improve on what already works. They do this with curiosity, persistence, and creativity. Engineers know how things work. For example, you can't fix a broken computer if you don't know how it functions. Just like engineers, leaders need to be problem solvers. Most election campaigns are based on issues people care about. Ideally, the candidate who shows a better understanding of the critical issues and presents a clear plan to solve them gets elected. If they want a second term, they must deliver on their initial promises to prove they can do it again.

Generally, every stage on the S-Curve has problems where the engineer metaphor may prove helpful. However, the engineer has to be your primary metaphor if your company is in decline and you want to turn it around.

The question is: Why not use the physician metaphor for diagnosis and problem-solving? After all, doctors don't just carry out checkups; they also treat ailments. Even though the human body is more consistent than the organizations we create, there's always a lengthy approval process before a medical treatment becomes mainstream. For instance, some people were reluctant to take COVID-19 vaccines because of the rushed approval process.[85] By contrast, there is more room for trial and error for engineers and leaders in problem-solving than for medical doctors.

So I recommend the physician metaphor for diagnosis. If the result is that the organization is facing significant issues, then use the engineer metaphor to solve them.

PROBLEM-SOLVING

What can leaders learn from engineers about problem-solving? Thankfully, I got the training and worked as a computer support engineer for many years. When I encounter a problem, I always start with the basics of how things work.

I once went on a temporary assignment to Gabon. Prior to my arrival, there was a problem that had existed for six months despite repeated attempts to fix it. All I did was reconnect the cable correctly, and it worked!

Perhaps my perspective was different because I wasn't involved with all the previous attempts. Anyway, it took me five minutes to get the server functioning again. We repeated the process three times

---

85   United Nations Children's Fund, "COVID-19 Vaccine Hesitancy," UNICEF, January 20, 2022, https://www.unicef.org/easterncaribbean/press-releases/covid-19-vaccine-hesitancy.

before the client reluctantly accepted my simple solution as a valid one.

The solution to a problem often doesn't have to be that complicated. Leaders need always to keep this in mind.

During leadership seminars, when we come to the engineer metaphor, I give basic puzzles for the participants to solve. I conclude the exercise by telling them, "You see, you can solve problems. You are already engineers!" It's a question of mindset. You need the mindset of an engineer when faced with a problem. Engineers see problems as opportunities. They don't run away from them. They keep trying until they solve them. Leaders need this mindset.

Unfortunately, not every problem has an easy solution. To save the company from bankruptcy following a record-setting corporate loss in 1993, IBM hired a new CEO, Louis V. Gerstner Jr. Mr. Gerstner recognized that culture, teamwork, customers, and leadership were "the elements that turned out to be the toughest challenges at IBM." He bluntly stated the management philosophy that helped him accomplish the dramatic turnaround of IBM despite the difficult challenges: "I look for people who work to solve problems and help colleagues. I sack politicians."[86]

Engineers see problems as opportunities.

Regardless of whether the problem is simple or complicated, always avoid the "cobra effect." This term rose to popularity in India decades ago when the British colonial government attempted to reduce the number of cobras in Delhi. Thinking incentives would help, they offered a bounty for every cobra killed. However, as soon as this went into effect, some savvy residents started breeding the snakes for income! The British realized this was a "perverse incentive" and

---

86   Louis V. Gerstner Jr., *Who Says Elephants Can't Dance?* (New York: Harper Business, December 16, 2003).

stopped the reward program. In turn, the cobra breeders released the now worthless but venomous snakes, thereby increasing their population—the opposite of what the British set out to do![87]

Leaders must avoid the cobra effect at all costs. They should solve problems, not make things worse. They must think carefully before implementing solutions.

CONTINUOUS IMPROVEMENT

The saying "If it isn't broke, don't fix it" may be accurate, but it doesn't mean engineers are idle when things are operational.

For example, there were over ten million black-and-white television sets in use when Scottish engineer John Logie Baird gave "the world's first demonstration of a practical fully electronic color television display" in August 1944.[88] Through continuous improvement, the TV has shifted from Baird's simple color image to ultrahigh-definition entertainment. This is how engineering works. It takes a concept that is good and continues to make enhancements. That's how leadership should also work—making improvements that compound over time to transform your organization into more remarkable accomplishments.

If you have an iPhone, compare your latest version with the first one that Apple released in 2007. You will notice a huge difference. These improvements didn't all happen at once. Every new model came with some improvements over the previous generation. This is what engineers do. They continuously improve on good products, so they

---

87   Wikipedia, "Perverse Incentive," last updated October 30, 2022, https://en.wikipedia. org/wiki/Perverse_incentive.

88   Wikipedia, "Color Television," last updated November 7, 2022, https://en.wikipedia. org/wiki/Color_television.

become even better. Leaders need to emulate engineers in this. They keep improving because that is how growth takes place.

Initially, it would take us two years at ISA to train newly hired engineers to the point that they were ready to implement projects on production sites. Since then, our recruitment and training processes have gone through several improvements. Now it takes not more than six months to get them fully ready. As you can see, you can practically improve on anything in your organization, whether a product, service, process, or procedure. There is no limit to improvement. It is a continuous process.

Another area of continuous improvement is your personal development as a leader. A stale leader stagnates the organization. What books are you reading? What training opportunities are you taking advantage of? The quest for learning took me to Harvard for the Owner/President Management (OPM) program and many other pieces of training I have taken over the years.

In addition, I use my driving time for personal development. If your commute time to and from work is one hour, you have enough time to listen to a whole book in one week. Giving allowance for holidays and distractions, with fifty-two weeks in a year, you can listen to at least twenty books.

With this approach, I've listened to many great books. My audiobook library now has hundreds of books on various topics: biographies of leaders, histories of nations and empires, science, and business. Yet my favorite is still the Bible. It contains several dozen books on numerous subjects, such as history, poetry, and prophecy. Most importantly, it is God's word. I recommend it for your regular reading and listening as a leader. As I explained earlier, I got the inspiration from the Bible to use familiar occupations as metaphors to simplify the understanding of leadership concepts, the core of *The Versatile Leader*.

IMPORTANT QUALITIES

How do engineers solve problems and improve things continuously? It is curiosity, persistence, and creativity. Some people are born with these qualities, but you can learn them also. That is why we have engineering schools. We shall take a closer look at these qualities because leaders need them too.

CURIOSITY

I always encourage younger engineers under training to avoid phrases such as "I think …" or "I believe …" when giving reports. Instead, I insist they must be curious and always ask more questions to find out how and why things work.

Leaders also need to be curious and show interest in how and why things function the way they do. Curiosity made Moses go closer when he "saw that though the bush was on fire it did not burn up." He went closer to investigate this strange sight. It turned out that his life and that of his enslaved people changed forever.[89] So I encourage leaders to be attentive to what is happening around them. However, be cautious with curiosity, for not all curiosity is good. As a young boy, I damaged my uncle's transistor radio set because I opened it up to find out how it worked. Fortunately, I didn't get spanked.

King Solomon spent enormous resources on his curiosity projects. He performed so many experiments and recorded his observations. Consider this passage from Ecclesiastes 2, where he wrote:

> I said to myself, "Come now, I will test you with pleasure to find out what is good." But that also proved to be meaningless. [2] "Laughter," I said, "is madness. And

---

89   Exodus 3.

what does pleasure accomplish?" [3] I tried cheering myself with wine, and embracing folly—my mind still guiding me with wisdom. I wanted to see what was good for people to do under the heavens during the few days of their lives. [4] I undertook great projects: I built houses for myself and planted vineyards. [5] I made gardens and parks and planted all kinds of fruit trees in them. [6] I made reservoirs to water groves of flourishing trees. [7] I bought male and female slaves and had other slaves who were born in my house. I also owned more herds and flocks than anyone in Jerusalem before me. [8] I amassed silver and gold for myself, and the treasure of kings and provinces. I acquired male and female singers, and a harem as well the delights of a man's heart. [9] I became greater by far than anyone in Jerusalem before me. In all this my wisdom stayed with me.

[10] I denied myself nothing my eyes desired;
 I refused my heart no pleasure.
My heart took delight in all my labor,
 and this was the reward for all my toil.
[11] Yet when I surveyed all that my hands had done
 and what I had toiled to achieve,
everything was meaningless, a chasing after the wind;
 nothing was gained under the sun.[90]

By his admission, Solomon's expensive experiments, with many pleasures of life, were a colossal waste! Leaders should avoid using their organization's resources for worthless experiments. As the old saying goes, "Curiosity killed the cat," and it can also kill a business.

---

90   Ecclesiastes 2:1–11.

PERSISTENCE

Some time ago, we went for scheduled preventive maintenance in one of our client's data centers. In simple terms, preventive maintenance means cleaning dust off computers. We would carry out these operations late in the evenings and on weekends when most people were not working. We started at 6:00 p.m. on this fateful day and were almost done by 8:00 p.m. To fully utilize the downtime, our client also planned maintenance of the electrical system during the same period. We finished our work successfully and turned the computers back on as usual. Our efforts were rewarded with fireworks this time, as if on New Year's Eve. Unfortunately, it wasn't a moment of celebration. The sparks were coming from the production servers! We were alarmed, but as engineers, we swung into action immediately.

Then, we checked and fixed the problem with the electrical system. Next, our objective was to get enough servers up and running so that all the hundred users could work the next day. We took components from some servers to fix the more critical ones. It took us the whole night, and by five o'clock the following day, we finally got the data center back in an operational state! In the end, we went home happy that we had persevered.

Persistence is what turns an impossible goal into an astounding reality. Nelson Mandela said, "Do not judge me by my successes; judge me by how many times I fell down and got back up again." That is persistence, pure and simple. After twenty-seven years in prison, he came out still focused on the same goal of ending the apartheid system in South Africa. No wonder South Africa became a free state in 1994. All leaders need this quality to achieve their critical goals.

Joshua's contemporary, Caleb, committed his adult life to one main goal: inheriting the promised land. Here's what he said at the age of eighty-five:

> Now then, just as the Lord promised, he has kept me alive for forty-five years since the time he said this to Moses, while Israel moved about in the wilderness. So here I am today, eighty-five years old! [11] I am still as strong today as the day Moses sent me out; I'm just as vigorous to go out to battle now as I was then. [12] Now give me this hill country that the Lord promised me that day. You yourself heard then that the Anakites were there and their cities were large and fortified, but, the Lord helping me, I will drive them out just as he said.[91]

Please note that Thomas Edison tried thousands of times before eventually inventing the light bulb. Leaders, please take note. In the face of such persistence, failure cannot endure.

CREATIVITY

Lessons from engineers are incomplete without creativity. We shall consider these three creativity levels: imitation, innovation, and invention.

Imitation is the starting point of creativity. A child learns by copying adults around them. When adults learn a new language, they speak like the people from the context where they learned it. Years ago, my Portuguese teacher, a native Portuguese speaker, found my accent quite amusing. She said I spoke with a typical Angolan accent, even though my level was elementary then. I had my first exposure to the

---

91   Joshua 14:10–12.

Portuguese language in Angola, so it is not surprising that she could detect my accent when I spoke. That's how imitation works, and it is not necessarily bad.

Mass production is another example of imitation. It is making many replicas of the masterpiece. If you can't copy your product, you can't increase production and, therefore, can't expand your business. When Samsung reported that they sold 2.5 million Galaxy Fold3 in 2021,[92] it means they copied their original Galaxy Fold3 2.5 million times. That's how it works; mass production is simply imitation.

Please beware: imitation has a poor reputation as a low-quality illegal copy. However, that's not always the case. Wal-Mart didn't invent its business model.[93] Also, the Japanese were shameless about copying. Niall Ferguson wrote:

> Ever since 1853–4, when their economy had been forcibly reopened to trade by the threatening "black ships" of the American Commodore Matthew C. Perry, the Japanese had struggled to work out what it was that made the West so much richer and stronger than the Rest. Touring the West—a practice so common that it inspired a sugoroku (board game)—only raised more questions. Was it their political system? Their educational institutions? Their culture? Or the way they dressed? Unsure, the Japanese decided to take no chances. They copied everything. From the Prussian-style constitution of 1889 to the adoption of the British gold standard in 1897, Japan's institutions

---

92   Ricci Rox, "Impressive Samsung Foldable Sales Pave Way for Galaxy Z Fold4 and Galaxy Z Flip4 Dominance," Notebookcheck.net, March 20, 2022, https://www. notebookcheck.net/Impressive-Samsung-foldable-sales-pave-way-for-Galaxy-Z-Fold4-and-Galaxy-Z-Flip4-dominance.609104.0.html.

93   Jim Collins, *How the Mighty Fall: And Why Some Companies Never Give In* (May 19, 2009).

were refashioned on Western models. The army drilled like Germans; the navy sailed like Britons. An American-style system of state elementary and middle schools was also introduced. The Japanese even started eating beef, hitherto taboo, and some reformers went so far as to propose abandoning Japanese in favour of English.[94]

Yes, leaders can imitate; they can copy, but must do so ethically.

The next two levels of creativity are innovation and invention. You need to innovate or invent if copying is unsuitable for practical or ethical reasons. I have grouped these two levels for two reasons. First, there's plenty of good literature on innovation, and I don't intend to bore you unnecessarily. Second, most of what is called an invention is nothing new.

Come to think of it, is the airplane an invention? The birds have flown since the beginning of time. So there's nothing new about flying. The Wright brothers did practically an imitation or, at best, an innovation that allows humans to do what birds always do effortlessly.

In any case, leaders need to find ways to achieve their strategic goals. They can innovate or invent if there are no good examples to imitate.

In conclusion, like engineers, leaders need to be curious, persistent, and creative as they try to solve significant problems and continuously improve themselves, their organizations, and society.

---

94   Niall Ferguson, *Civilization: The West and the Rest* (New York: Penguin Books, October 30, 2012).

CHAPTER 8

ENTREPRENEUR

Better an honest failure than a fake success.

—AFRICAN PROVERB

So far, in this strategy part of *The Versatile Leader*, we have seen that the physician metaphor helps the leader in diagnosing their organization and deciding on what to do next. If the organization is new, the architect metaphor helps in envisioning its desired future. A company that is healthy and ready to grow needs a builder to nurture it to maturity. Finally, if the diagnosis shows significant problems, the leader should use the engineer metaphor to solve them.

However, in any situation, the leader must use the entrepreneur metaphor to produce tangible results. Regarding results, Gino Wickman wrote, "Entrepreneurs create the most jobs, are a driving force in the economy, possess a large portion of the wealth, and spearhead much of the innovation that changes the world."[95]

As a leader, I believe you have important goals. Even if you don't aim to change the world, you can learn great lessons from entrepre-

---

95   Gino Wickman, *Entrepreneurial Leap* (Dallas, TX: BenBella Books, October 22, 2019).

neurs. You will understand from them the meaning of ownership and optimism that will help you in your undertakings. You'll also learn to take calculated risks and bring about substantial outcomes.

OWNERSHIP

"Ownership really starts with what's not yours!" It's something my dad helped me understand in my childhood. In those days, my dad would send us, his children, to run errands. Sometimes we would complain, and he would say, "It's okay, you may leave it. It is for your own benefit that I am sending you on this errand."

This statement always left me wondering. What good would it serve me for Uncle Tarwa to have yet another meeting with my father? Though I found it confusing, I wouldn't ask. Fortunately, one day my dad explained. He said, "If you refuse to run errands for me now, in the future, you will also give excuses for what is yours."

I didn't fully grasp what he meant then, but after many years, the lesson became clear. Dad was teaching me a powerful lesson on ownership.

Ownership is a mindset, not a status. You don't need your name on a share certificate to take responsibility for getting things done in your company. You don't need a bonus to think and act for the good of everyone in the organization. Leaders need to learn and internalize this entrepreneurial trait.

Many years ago, I had already internalized my dad's ownership lesson. As a service delivery manager, we were working on a proposal for an important project for one of our clients. Late one evening, my **Ownership is a mindset, not a status.** colleague and sales manager reminded me of the difference between our two jobs. He said he would get the bonus no matter what I did. I answered that the bonus was not the reason I did my job. Furthermore, it didn't matter to me who got one. Nothing would change the way I did my job.

Leaders must learn from entrepreneurs how to work for the best outcomes for their organizations—even if they will not get any direct benefits. Please, don't get me wrong. I am not in any way advocating that people work for free. On the contrary, as an entrepreneur, I can say that profit is a legitimate motive. My point here is that short-term personal benefit does not automatically imply responsibility. Paying you more money won't necessarily make you more productive.

Those who have learned to work with responsibility regardless of immediate benefits are ready to start and run their businesses. I have noticed this as I meet regularly with two young friends of mine, Fatima Almeida and Mario Goldinho. In the few years I have known them, both have impressed me with their deep sense of ownership and dedication. They have been working on their start-up and have made some significant progress. BayQi.com is an e-commerce platform that enables everyone, including people without proper addresses, to make online purchases and collect them at specific points in their neighborhood (which they call BayQiPoints).

Fatima and Mario are pouring everything they have into this start-up. I do not doubt in my mind that, with that kind of commitment, they will succeed. While mentoring them, I have found that I am also learning, as I watch them talk about changing lives with their powerful financial inclusion ideas.

Please visit an entrepreneur and observe their enthusiasm. Then, take the lessons you have learned and apply them to your relevant leadership situation. That seems to be what God asked the prophet Jeremiah to do:

This is the word that came to Jeremiah from the Lord: ² "Go down to the potter's house, and there I will give you my message." ³ So I went down to the potter's house, and I saw him working at the wheel. ⁴ But the pot he was shaping from the clay was marred in his hands; so the potter formed it into another pot, shaping it as seemed best to him. ⁵ Then the word of the Lord came to me. ⁶ He said, "Can I not do with you, Israel, as this potter does?" declares the Lord. "Like clay in the hand of the potter, so are you in my hand, Israel."⁹⁶

Jeremiah, a prophet, went to a potter to learn lessons included in his subsequent prophecy. So I urge you to learn from the entrepreneurs around you. Carefully watch their incredible sense of responsibility and optimism, which will help you achieve more as a leader.

OPTIMISM

The US National Academy of Science released a study on optimism. It states that "optimism is specifically related to 11 to 15 percent longer life span."⁹⁷ Therefore, optimism is an excellent thing for every leader to have.

This raises the question, Is it possible to learn optimism? Yes, it is, and don't take my word for it. Martin E. P. Seligman, professor of psychology, wrote a book titled *Learned Optimism: How to Change Your Mind and Your Life*. The title alone says what the book is all about. Once again, it is possible to learn optimism.

---

96   Jeremiah 18:1–6.

97   Lewina O. Lee et al., "Optimism Is Associated with Exceptional Longevity in 2 Epidemiologic Cohorts of Men and Women," *PNAS* 116, no. 37 (August 26, 2019), https://doi.org/10.1073/pnas.1900712116.

The second question is this: From whom should you learn optimism? Entrepreneurs, of course. I am convinced that no other group is as optimistic as entrepreneurs. This is confirmed by another study published by Tinbergen Institute, noting what we have known all along—that entrepreneurs are generally more optimistic than others.[98] Therefore, leaders who choose to learn this quality from entrepreneurs may add some years to their life span!

Now, let's talk about the other side of the spectrum, pessimism. Based on his years of research, Professor Martin notes that "pessimists can transform mere setbacks into disasters."

Take Hugo, who worked in one of our partner organizations. He wasn't starting with a setback and had a good job. Unfortunately, thoughts of being fired were constantly on his mind. I even heard him joking about this on more than one occasion. Eventually, his self-fulfilling prophecy became a reality, forcing him to find employment elsewhere.

Optimists are different people and see setbacks as opportunities to learn and grow. They can transform disasters into excellent outcomes for many people. A Nigerian soccer star, Nwankwo Kanu, did just that.

Nwankwo Kanu was the captain of the Nigerian soccer team. He led the team to win the gold medal at the Olympics in 1996. Soon after his return from the Olympics, Kanu was diagnosed with a severe heart defect, and doctors believed that his career as a soccer player was over. However, he underwent successful heart surgery and eventually returned to active sports. "Kanu's experience also led to his founding the Kanu Heart Foundation, an organization that helps predomi-

---

98   Martin Koudstaal, Randolph Sloof, and Mirjam van Praag, "Are Entrepreneurs More Optimistic and Overconfident Than Managers and Employees?," Tinbergen Institute discussion paper 15-124/VII, November 5, 2015, available at SSRN: https://ssrn.com/abstract=2687101.

nantly young African children who suffer heart defects and whose work was expanded to provide aid for homeless children in 2008."[99] So the career-ending, life-threatening ailment has been turned into a foundation that is saving many lives. It takes optimism to do that. That's precisely what every leader needs.

Even if you are generally inclined to pessimism, you can learn what Professor Martin calls "disputation." You can use disputation to argue against your pessimistic tendencies, overcome obstacles, and achieve positive outcomes.

A great example of this concept comes from Matthew 15:21–28. A Canaanite woman came to Jesus, telling him that her daughter was "demon-possessed and suffering terribly." At first, Jesus's disciples encouraged him to send her away because she was bothering them. Yet this woman ignored their warnings and didn't stop, even when Jesus issued what sounded like a condescending comment: "I was sent only to the lost sheep of Israel."

Instead of being offended and going away, this woman came and knelt in front of Jesus, presenting her request, "Lord, help me!" Most pessimists would consider Jesus's subsequent comment nasty and walk away for good.

He said, "It is not right to take the children's bread and toss it to the dogs."

Rather than give up in disgust, the woman turned this imminent setback to her advantage. "Yes, it is, Lord," she said. "Even the dogs eat the crumbs that fall from their master's table."

Then Jesus said to her, "Woman, you have great faith! Your request is granted." And her daughter was healed at that moment!

---

99   Wikipedia, "Nwankwo Kanu," last updated November 8, 2022, https://en.wikipedia.org/wiki/Nwankwo_Kanu.

Wasn't Jesus too hard with this woman? You may say so, but I think he saw something in her that he wanted to draw out for everyone to see. An exceptional optimism that Jesus called "great faith." It is something that leaders also should have.

This encounter is an excellent example of optimistic disputation that can turn imminent disaster into a great outcome. That's what leaders need.

Even if you are a natural optimist, sometimes negative thoughts can hit you suddenly like armed bandits. This is what happened to me several years ago. After a frustrating encounter with government inspectors, I was exhausted. I was discouraged and angry. Many negative thoughts filled my mind. I wondered if it was worth it to continue in business. Then, for some reason, I decided to go to my internet browser and search for a pair of contrasting words: "good" and "evil," and "success" and "failure," and "love" and "hate." I was astonished by what I found. For each pair, the positive word had more hits than the negative word! For example, as of this writing, Google search reports 3,100,000,000 hits for "optimism" compared to 436,000,000 hits for "pessimism." Put differently, there are seven times more resources on optimism than pessimism! You can also find about seven times more resources on "good" than "evil." And "success" is at least 1.5 times more popular than "failure."

I concluded that the world is much more positive than I felt. Motivated by my findings, I created a training program called "Success Unmasked." I've since used it to teach hundreds of people how they can have authentic success.

Sometime later, at the end of one training session in Huambo, central Angola, a woman gave feedback that the training saved her marriage! She had plans to divorce her husband, but she changed her mind during the training. Marriage wasn't part of what we covered. That was simply an unexpected but pleasant outcome.

A few years later, during another session in Bloemfontein, South Africa, a well-known criminal in the area came into the venue. The way the participants looked over their shoulders, I could tell something was not right. In the end, the guy made a public commitment to live a new life of faith as a Christian! Something I didn't expect would happen at all. It wasn't planned to be part of the program, but it happened.

I can't take credit for any of these events. One thing I can say for sure is that on that day, I almost quit; I had a breakthrough. Pessimism was defeated when I realized it wasn't that powerful. Optimism won a decisive victory against pessimism by a factor of seven.

When you, as a leader, understand that optimism can overcome setbacks and adversity, you are ready to take risks in pursuit of results that matter.

RISK-TAKING

Do entrepreneurs take risks thoughtlessly? Not at all. Successful entrepreneurs manage their risks carefully. They only take risks if, after careful analysis, they realize they have an advantage and can get a good outcome.

In our company's early years, we would ask these two questions: "What if it fails?" and "What if it works?" That would give us opposing views of the possible outcomes of the risks we were about to take.

We once wanted to acquire a property for our company headquarters. In those days, rent was skyrocketing, and Luanda was rated the most expensive city in the world.[100] Consequently, it was a strategic objective for us to own the buildings we needed to run our business. Unfortunately, the cost of buying a property was also high. We needed a mortgage, but it was difficult to obtain one. Our bank was willing to give us a loan, but we had to pay it back within thirty-six months, and monthly installments would be a considerable stretch for our finances.

What if we failed and defaulted on the repayments? The bank would seize the property, and we would lose money and our reputation. That was scary.

On the other hand, what if it worked? We would have an asset for our business that would give us room to grow without paying exorbitant rent. The property could also serve as collateral for future loans—leverage that would be important for our growth.

After carefully analyzing our cash flow and sales pipeline, we decided to go ahead with the loan to acquire the property. It was a considerable risk, but it was a risk worth taking. We purchased the property in Bairro Azul, a good area of the city of Luanda. That property continues to serve as our headquarters to this day.

Entrepreneurs do not always see a great result every time they take a risk. Sometimes the result can be disastrous. I have started over a dozen businesses in less than two decades, most of which have failed. This is to say a risk worth taking doesn't guarantee a good result.

The leadership lesson here is that in analyzing risk, focus not just on the spectacular results but also the consequences of failure. Similarly, weigh your risk appetite against your risk capacity. Those who focus exclusively on the positive side may take risks above their capacity with disastrous outcomes. Jim Collins wrote:

---

100   Louise Redvers, "Living in the World's Most Expensive City," BBCNews.com, February 2, 2012, https://www.bbc.com/news/business-16815605.

It's hard to argue that the primary cause of the Wall Street meltdowns of 2008 lay in a lack of drive or ambition; if anything, people went too far—too much risk, too much leverage, too much financial innovation, too much aggressive opportunism, too much growth.[101]

On the other hand, those who are so fixated on the negative side will bury many good opportunities. For this reason, Europeans say, "Nothing ventured, nothing gained." But Africans say, "A dog will not eat a bone tied to a snake." With these two opposite perspectives or using a different risk analysis approach, a leader can analyze wisely and take risks to achieve desired results—results that matter.

RESULTS

To remain in business, an entrepreneur needs results. Therefore, profit is an essential bottom line of an entrepreneurial venture. Without profit, a business venture will fail. Entrepreneurs know that a reasonable profit gives them financial independence. Therefore, they work very hard to achieve it. In *Built to Last*, Jim Collins said, "Profit is like oxygen, food, water, and blood for the body; they are not the point of life, but without them, there is no life."

He further stated that visionary companies "pursue profits. And yes, they pursue broader, more meaningful ideals."[102] There are reasons they do that. In my company, for example, in a recent survey, only about 5 percent of the participants directly or indirectly mentioned money as a critical factor. Instead, most participants talked about values often overlooked in the work environment, such as love, social justice, fairness, and honesty.

---

101 Jim Collins, *How the Mighty Fall*.

102 Jim Collins, *Built to Last*.

As a leader of a business venture, please ensure you have the oxygen (profit) that allows you to breathe and pursue more meaningful ideals.

What are my ideals as an entrepreneur and a leader? Interestingly, I answered a similar question from auditors quite recently. The fact that we can provide professional services to our clients that are comparable to the high standards found anywhere in the world is very satisfying to me. To see people grow in their careers gives me great joy. Seeing them achieve more than they thought possible is even more fulfilling. For me, a company is an environment where I see these things happen repeatedly.

Regardless of the type of organization you are leading, there are ideals far beyond profit, position, and power that you should pursue as a leader. What are they? That is the question each leader must answer. If your goals are such that you can't really talk about them with your staff, customers, or electoral constituency, then there is an alignment problem.

To deliver results that matter to all your important stakeholders, you should engage them in your leadership ideals. Of course, people want to be part of such ideals. They want to be part of something much bigger than your company's net profit. They want to make a difference in the world.

Please lead them like an entrepreneur. Lead them with responsibility and optimism. Don't be afraid to take risks when required to obtain results that matter. Also, ensure that your ideals are worth the commitment of others.

PART III

TACTICS

CHAPTER 9

JOURNALIST

It's better to be punished for telling the truth
than to be rewarded for telling lies.
—AFRICAN PROVERB

In part II, we examined strategy metaphors. These are metaphors with profound impact, even though you may not use them frequently. In this section (part III), we shall look at metaphors for tactics. Depending on the situation, you will always need at least one of these metaphors daily. However, they require defined objectives for them to function efficiently. Without a strategy, your tactical efforts may not generate meaningful value.

As with the strategy section, getting reliable information is where tactics start. Essentially, the journalist metaphor does for tactics what the physician does for strategy. The main difference is that the journalist metaphor is for obtaining information for day-to-day operations. In contrast, the physician metaphor is for diagnosing the organization's strategic situation. However, both must make truthful assessments.

Journalists remind us that a good decision not conveyed properly may not realize its intended objective. Therefore, leaders can learn from journalists how to communicate clearly and confidently with stakeholders.

As with other metaphors, you can learn many different things from journalists, but obtaining reliable information and keeping others informed are the two that are relevant here.

RELIABLE INFORMATION

Great journalists are obsessed with obtaining reliable information. I witnessed this in 2013 when Nelson Mandela was near the end of his life. At age ninety-five, Mandela's remaining days on this earth were few, and journalists anticipated his passing any day. To this point, South African journalist Rian Malan wrote this fascinating account:

> I just called my pal Colin, a TV news cameraman who has been parked for days outside the Pretoria hospital where Nelson Mandela is being treated … Then we started talking about how much this is costing world media, especially the American TV networks … Every time Mandela goes into hospital, large numbers of Americans (up to fifty) are flown here to take up their positions, and the South African network is similarly activated. Colin, for instance, travels to Johannesburg, hires a car, and checks into a hotel, all on the network's ticket. Since last December, he's probably spent close to thirty days (at $2,000 a day, expenses included) cooling his heels at various poolsides. And he has yet to shoot a single frame … Meanwhile, the military doctors tending the royal bed are saying absolutely nothing useful about the old man's condition. All we know with certainty this afternoon is that Colin has been ordered to stand down again—perhaps because his

employers are hemorrhaging so badly that they're likely to die before Mandela dies.[103]

On December 5, 2013, the South African government made the much-anticipated announcement, and journalists reported Nelson Mandela's death to the world. This behind-the-scenes look into the world of journalism raised the question, Why do news outlets spend so much time, money, and effort in this manner?

There is a long-held belief in journalism that accuracy depends on the narrator's proximity to the scene of the action. This was the case years ago when "transmitting news was by word of mouth."[104] Great journalists want to be first on the scene and have firsthand eyewitnesses to the event they are reporting. This keeps them from leaning on secondhand information that may miss some essential details.

Leaders should likewise do their best to glean information personally. They should be close enough to the action that they can hear from primary sources.

However, there are moments when it is impossible to be at the scene of action. One example was when my technical team performed a major upgrade of critical systems for one of our customers. It was a crucial operation, and I needed to know what was happening.

Unfortunately, there was no way I could be there personally. At the end of the operation, my team reported great success. But the customer's perspective was different—not everything went well.

If you watch TV interviews, you will notice that good journalists ask many questions and do not make any assumptions. They even ask questions when they are already quite sure of the answer.

103　Rian Malan, "The Vultures Waiting for Nelson Mandela's Death," https://www.spectator.co.uk/ (The Spectator, June 26, 2013), https://www.spectator.co.uk/article/the-vultures-waiting-for-nelson-mandela-s-death/.

104　Sarah Niblock, *Journalism: A Beginner's Guide* (London: Oneworld Publications, February 1, 2010).

Leaders ought to do the same. It is better to discard assumptions and biases when trying to obtain information. Ask questions and carefully listen to the answers. This requires much patience, especially when the answers are long and you do not have much time. Please remember that "he who asks questions cannot avoid answers."[105]

Getting reliable information on an ongoing basis is an essential aspect of the leader's job. David Packard, cofounder and one-time CEO of HP, noted, "Our visits always included a walk around the facilities, giving us the opportunity to meet and chat informally with our employees and see the work they were doing."[106] This management concept that Packard used has been named "management by walking around (MBWA)." Leaders can learn MBWA best with the journalist metaphor. Journalists are generally on the move, chasing stories to wherever they may take them. Leaders should act similarly.

Toyota has a similar concept called Gemba. "Going to the Gemba means observing firsthand how our products are being designed, built, used, and what problems we have," said Akio Toyoda, president of Toyota.[107]

Therefore, journalists and leaders need firsthand information in a similar way. The challenge is how do you get firsthand information these days when working from home has become the norm?

VIRTUAL INFORMATION

In their traditional sense, Management by Walking Around and Gemba wouldn't help you much in a virtual work setting. As a leader, you still need reliable information to make sound decisions.

---

105 African (Cameroonian) proverb.
106 David Packard, *The HP Way*.
107 Jeffrey K. Liker, *The Toyota Way*.

In the words of Sarah Niblock, "Every new media format carries issues as well as opportunities for journalism."[108] I believe this concept also applies to leaders. Leaders can take full advantage of social media to obtain necessary information.

Anil Varghese, operations manager of Vallantis, is great at making sense of social media statuses. For example, when he sees a change in my social media status that he considers essential, he checks on me to find out what is happening. One such call came when I used a hand-drawn map of Africa as my WhatsApp profile picture. I used it because I was impressed with my daughter's beautiful rendering of the continent.

In many respects, Anil uses social media as an extended form of Management by Walking Around.

In today's culture, journalists monitor social media such as Twitter and Facebook posts for important information, illustrating that the Gemba is not just the factory floor but also LinkedIn, Twitter, Facebook, and blog posts!

Leaders need to adapt to the internet revolution. However, they must also be aware of privacy issues as lines are often blurred between personal, private, public, and official information. A humorous example occurred when Analise Ferreira, our head of operations, brought to my attention something worrisome. Our senior engineer, Martinho Reis, had an updated LinkedIn status that said "#OPEN-TOWORK." Although we respected his privacy, we were concerned he might be looking for other employment opportunities. Meanwhile, he seemed happy in his current position. As it turned out, this step wasn't deliberate. Martinho simply responded to questions during his profile update and was unaware that LinkedIn had shown him as someone looking for work!

---

108   Sarah Niblock, *Journalism*.

In essence, the principle of spontaneously checking on your team members can still happen today, even when your coworkers are working remotely. Social media statuses and posts can indicate what may be happening in their lives. Also, informal conversations during videoconferences can serve as MBWA. When you combine these with tones in voice calls and emails, you can still obtain reliable information that will help you effectively lead your remote and virtual teams.

Please remember that as important as information gathering is, it is not an end. What you do with it is of greater importance.

REPORTING

Great journalists work hard to obtain reliable information from different sources. They then organize and deliver their findings to their audience, allowing them to form their own opinions.

Leaders handle the information they have gathered a bit differently than journalists. First, they use the information they collect to make decisions and act in the interest of their organizations. Then they convey those actions and decisions to the stakeholders or the public.

Please remember that as important as information gathering is, it is not an end. What you do with it is of greater importance.

So the information leaders give out is not necessarily tied to the information they have collected.

A journalist may gather tons of information, but she hasn't done her job if she does not file a report. News reporting is what people look for. Journalists use a variety of ways to report information. One that is of particular interest to me is the documentary. Betsy Chasse noted, "More people want not only to share real stories but to hear and watch them."[109] Leaders can learn from journalists how to write "real stories" for their stakeholders.

During my career, I've written many reports. Since I work a lot with engineers, I've also read a lot of technical reports. I always advise engineers to be considerate of their audience. You may impress yourself with much technical jargon, but in the end, the reader is not you. You will achieve your purpose if the recipient reads, makes sense, and takes the desired action. If your audience cannot understand your writing, you have wasted your time and theirs.

One report I particularly like writing is a handover report. These short summaries help me reflect more than any other type of report. During handover reports, I aim to make it as easy as possible for the person coming after me to function at ease. One example was when I was handing over my volunteer role in our church as a chairperson of the elders' council. I realized our church didn't have a written history, so I took some weeks to investigate and wrote the first draft of our history as part of my handover notes.

Keeping good personal records will help you base your written reports on facts, not fiction. In addition, there are moments when you need to speak to your stakeholders. You can also learn from journalists how to do that effectively.

PRESS BRIEFING

Leaders can also learn from journalists by the way they conduct press briefings. Many public officeholders have ways of informing the public of what they do. For example, the office of the president of the United States does it daily through the White House press briefings.

---

109 Betsy Chasse, *The Documentary Filmmaking Master Class* (New York: Allworth, November 19, 2019).

It has a straightforward format. First, the White House press secretary summarizes what has happened since the last briefing to a select group of journalists. Then, a question-and-answer session. Similarly, every leader needs to find a way of "briefing" their constituency even if they don't have a press secretary. This does not need to be daily or lengthy. The key is to disseminate helpful information in an ongoing manner.

At ISA, we have a monthly staff meeting during which we summarize what has happened in the last month. Since we do not have a press secretary, the human resources (HR) department coordinates this meeting. It allows everyone in the company to get to know what is happening and ask questions. We try to keep the duration of our staff meetings to no more than one hour.

Sometimes, news cannot wait for scheduled briefings or broadcasts and must go out immediately as the event occurs. This is true for both journalists and leaders. The news media calls such breaking news.

BREAKING NEWS

We can take this lesson from everyday life. For example, when a child is born, parents don't wait for a regular family meeting to tell everyone the good news. Likewise, the bad news is shared immediately when someone in the family dies.

Breaking news or a news flash "is a current issue that broadcasters feel warrants the interruption of scheduled programming or current news in order to report its details."[110]

For example, when Will Smith slapped Chris Rock on stage at the Oscars in 2022, many news outlets broadcasted the infamous act as breaking news.

---

110 Wikipedia, "Breaking News," last updated October 18, 2022, https://en.wikipedia.org/wiki/Breaking_news.

Leaders can learn from journalists how to share certain news in their organization as they occur. For example, when Total Energies awarded ISA a major project in 2020, we did not wait for our regular staff meeting. Instead, we immediately informed everyone in the company and the partners who worked with us in the tendering process.

Leaders need to decide what constitutes breaking news in their organization. Of course, it doesn't always have to be good news. However, all relevant information should be truthfully communicated to relevant stakeholders.

FAKE NEWS

Good journalism is good for society in many ways. Sadly, some journalists are willing to misrepresent the truth for various reasons. Unfortunately, fake news is not something new.

In the Bible, the book of 2 Samuel chapter 18 records the tragic end to Absalom's rebellion against his father, King David. In the final battle against his father's army led by Joab, Absalom's long hair got caught up in the branches of an oak tree. He was left hanging in midair. When Joab got there, he finished Absalom off with three spears. Of course, the rebellion ended.

This breaking news event was significant for King David. In that age, instant communication from a long distance was not possible. Instead, the information had to be carried by word of mouth. Like a true journalist, Ahimaaz, son of Zadok, wanted to report the news to the king, but Joab didn't allow him. "You aren't the one to bring the news today. You can bring news on another day, but not today, because the king's son is dead,"[111] Joab responded.

---

111   2 Samuel 18:20 CEV.

Joab changed his mind when Ahimaaz was adamant that he must personally carry the news of the military triumph to the king. Ahimaaz then ran past the Cushite, the other reporter, using a different route. Like Usain Bolt, he charged past the finish line to win the race.

When Ahimaaz came to King David, like every skilled journalist, he began with the headlines, "We won! We won!"[112]

Unfortunately, King David was not excited. David was more worried about the safety of his rebellious son, Absalom. The king asked, "Is the young man Absalom safe?"

Ahimaaz then understood why Joab wasn't eager to allow him to carry the news. He answered the king. "I saw a large crowd right when Joab, the king's servant, sent your servant off, but I don't know what it was about."

Regrettably, Ahimaaz resorted to misinformation when he saw that an accurate report could enrage the king. Fortunately, the second journalist delivered the accurate news. Understandably, Ahimaaz was worried about his safety. David had passed death sentences on two similar occasions in the past. The person who reported the death of King Saul, David's predecessor, met his untimely death. Then, the two men who murdered King Saul's son and came to report, thinking they would get a reward from David, suffered the same fate. So Ahimaaz had reasons to be afraid.

However, is there no other way to report the news despite the safety concerns without telling lies? Should a journalist turn to falsehood because of risks?

Despite its apparent benefits, misinformation is terrible for journalists and leaders. As the late Larry King, the popular radio and television host, said, "Be honest. You can never go wrong, in broad-

---

112   2 Samuel 18:28 CEV.

casting or in any area of speech."[113] As leaders, we must find ways of telling people the truth, even if it is bad news. Unfortunately, that is not what is happening in our society today.

According to the 2022 Edelman Trust Barometer, 76 percent of people internationally surveyed "worry about false information or fake news."[114] Most of the fake news is circulated informally on social media. The same Edelman Trust Barometer in 2017 "reveals that trust is in crisis around the world. The general population's trust in the institutions of business, government, NGOs [nongovernmental organizations], and media declined broadly."[115] The lack of trust in the official institutions made many seek informal sources of information that have now become breeding grounds for fake news.

This is a warning to every leader. It should remind us that tinkering with the facts to make a quick sale undermines credibility, a critical leadership asset. No amount of propaganda will save a sinking leader that has lost credibility. The best way out is to go back to the old narrow way of telling the truth in plain language.

---

113   Larry King and Bill Gilbert, *How to Talk to Anyone, Anytime, Anywhere: The Secrets of Good Communication* (New York: Crown, October 24, 1995).

114   Edelman, "2022 Edelman Trust Barometer," accessed November 14, 2022, https://www.edelman.com/trust/2022-trust-barometer.

115   Edelman, "2017 Edelman Trust Barometer," accessed November 14, 2022, https://www.edelman.com/trust/2017-trust-barometer

CHAPTER 10

COACH

There is always a winner, even in a monkey's beauty contest.
—AFRICAN PROVERB

The journalist metaphor helps us understand what is going on in our organizations. However, the question of what to do with our findings remains. In the following three chapters, we shall examine some metaphors that will help you lead with confidence in a broad range of internal situations. The first of these is the metaphor coach.

Coaches teach us how to select and train teams. They teach us the importance of topics such as delegation and competition. As the business author Jack Stack notes in *The Great Game of Business*, "Business is a game to be played where there are real winners and losers."[116]

While I consider myself a passive football fan, one can't miss this popular game living in Africa. I have learned so much over the years watching soccer matches.

---

116 Jack Stack and Bo Burlingham, *The Great Game of Business, Expanded and Updated: The Only Sensible Way to Run a Company* (New York: Crown, 2013).

SELECTION

In preparing for significant tournaments such as the FIFA World Cup, coaches go everywhere looking for the best talents for their teams. In the same way, leaders should take this aspect of their job very seriously.

Jesus chose his team with great care. Luke 6:12–13 records how he went about this: "One of those days Jesus went out to a mountainside to pray and spent the night praying to God. When morning came, he called his disciples to him and chose twelve of them, whom he also designated apostles." We should also handle selection with utmost care to avoid having the wrong players who may ruin our organizations.

Founder and CEO of Pleasure Travels, Paul Ubwa, said, "Competence is easier to train, so I watch out more for attitude."[117] He provided one example of how he spotted great talent during the hiring process.

Paul wanted to hire a mechanic to care for his growing fleet of vehicles. One of the applicants was a man named Moses. On the day Paul conducted his interviews, Moses got there very early. When he arrived, Moses joined Paul to clear the debris at the workshop under repair. Since they hadn't met before, Paul thought Moses was one of the temporary laborers brought in for a project.

Later, when Moses went in for the interview, Paul recognized him as the person who had helped clean up the rubble moments earlier. The interview was over before it began. Moses had the job! Rolling up his sleeves to work on something that had nothing to do with his work area was a good indicator of his virtue. Years later, Paul has never regretted that decision, as Moses has consistently performed his duties above and beyond his expectations.

---

117   Paul Ubwa, personal communication, April 18, 2022.

Every leader needs to learn from Paul that character and competence are both important, but as the saying goes, "Man's only real possession is his character."

TRAINING

After selecting people to be part of your team, you still have much work to do for them to deliver good outcomes for your organization. Coaches are often referred to as trainers because training is the central aspect of their job. It indeed requires patience, time, and effort. Therefore, coaching at a professional level is a full-time occupation.

During the early months of my first job, when I was still inexperienced and couldn't work independently, my boss contracted an experienced consultant named Dimeji to implement projects and train me. Working with Dimeji gave me valuable exposure that I wouldn't have otherwise. So many things I learned from him helped me in my career. However, it was also clear that the problem-solving methods that worked for him were unsuitable for my personality, and I had to develop my techniques.

This experience taught me that coaching is not the same as cloning. You cannot make your trainees a replica of yourself, so there is no point in trying. If human cloning becomes possible or legally permitted, coaches and leaders will never be specialists in this area. Therefore, leaders must learn from great coaches and train people as unique individuals. They must train them to understand the fundamentals and then give them the freedom to unleash their creativity. Doing so is good for you, them, and your organization.

Regardless of their roles, train your personnel in operations and leadership. There are many advantages: they can do a lot more by themselves, you can delegate to them, and they experience growth.

DELEGATION

Delegation is a vital concept in both management and coaching. Delegation is the transfer of responsibility for tasks, functions, or decisions from one person to another.[118] It is not a replacement or blame "transfer channel." It is also not the same in every situation.

Good coaches don't criticize things they don't understand. Similarly, leaders should be careful to observe before advising.

During important soccer competitions, coaches must stay outside the pitch. In other words, coaches must trust the players with the success or failure of their clubs. When the players lose, the coaches lose. When they win, the coaches celebrate. Rather than engaging in the game physically, coaches must instead stand on the sidelines and watch—doing their best not to allow their blood to boil! Leaders must learn this important skill from coaches.

If done correctly, delegation can help prevent burnout. This was Jethro's point to Moses as he led the newly liberated people of Israel. Having watched his schedule, Jethro taught:[119]

> [17] What you are doing is not good. [18] You and these people who come to you will only wear yourselves out. The work is too heavy for you; you cannot handle it alone. [19] Listen now to me and I will give you some advice, and may God be with you. You must be the people's representative before God and bring their disputes to him. [20] Teach them his decrees and instructions, and show them the way they

---

118   Wikipedia, "Delegation," last updated September 2, 2022, https://en.wikipedia.org/wiki/Delegation.

119   Exodus 18.

are to live and how they are to behave. [21] But select capable men from all the people—men who fear God, trustworthy men who hate dishonest gain—and appoint them as officials over thousands, hundreds, fifties and tens. [22] Have them serve as judges for the people at all times, but have them bring every difficult case to you; the simple cases they can decide themselves. That will make your load lighter, because they will share it with you. [23] If you do this and God so commands, you will be able to stand the strain, and all these people will go home satisfied.

Note that Jethro watched before he counseled his son-in-law on delegation. Good coaches don't criticize things they don't understand. Similarly, leaders should be careful to observe before advising.

Let us now consider these three fundamental levels of delegation—basic, intermediate, and high:

- **Basic level:** This level is suitable for some new hires and low-skilled positions requiring high guidance. Assign tasks to the person with instructions to follow. They report back, and you decide what to do next.
- **Intermediate level:** At this level, assign goals for team members to report at the end of the assignment. If you are comfortable with their recommendations, approve implementation. A team member with a proven track record can move to the next level.
- **High level:** This level is for team members who have consistently demonstrated competence at the previous level. They can take on new challenges and carry out new projects without needing their manager to intervene. They can set their own and other people's goals and can act independently.

They typically submit their reports to inform. You must be careful rushing people to a high level of delegation.

TIME MANAGEMENT

Time affects everything in this life. Competitive sports teach us that you can't take even a second for granted.

One soccer match brought a time management lesson to the forefront. It was an Olympics semifinal match between Nigeria and Brazil in Atlanta, Georgia, on July 31, 1996. The highly rated and favored side, Brazil, was leading 3-1 well into the second half. Most people had lost hope but not the Dutchman Johannes Bonfrere, the coach of the Nigerian team. He made a substitution in the seventy-fifth minute. By the seventy-eighth minute, Nigeria scored its second goal, giving some hope. Both sides hotly contested the remaining twelve minutes. Nigeria's side scored its equalizing goal by the ninetieth minute (literally the last minute)! The Nigerian captain, Nwankwo Kanu, scored the winning goal (golden goal) by the ninety-fourth minute, qualifying for the finals.[120]

As you can see from the above story, in competition, winning and losing are determined by a measure of time. Being a good coach also means you must be good at time management. You need to time your changes and substitutions correctly. Leaders can learn from good coaches how to make every minute count for their organizations.

In athletics, it is even more evident. According to Guinness World Records, "Arguably the most iconic of all records was broken by Usain Bolt in 2009 when the Jamaican runner completed the fastest 100

---

120 Wikipedia, "Nigeria at the 1996 Summer Olympics," last updated January 9, 2022, https://en.wikipedia.org/wiki/Nigeria_at_the_1996_Summer_Olympics.

meters ever, in a ground-breaking time of 9.58 seconds."[121] Second to Usain is Tyson Gay, who holds the number two record. According to Sports Unfold, Tyson completed 100 meters in 9.69 seconds.[122]

As you can see, seconds make all the difference. Learn from coaches and athletes how to manage your time for remarkable results because every second is truly important.

Those who manage businesses are aware that late filing of taxes can lead to penalties. Also, submitting your proposal late may disqualify you from an important bidding process. Good leaders do not need external constraints to value their time. They set their goals and timelines and do what it takes to achieve them as if they were running for gold at the Olympic Games.

SPORTSMANSHIP

On January 23, 2004, a Namibian soccer team, KK Palace, played against F.C. Civics Windhoek during a national championship competition. The full-time play ended in a 2-2 draw. This soccer match with forty-eight kicks found its way into the *Guinness Book of Records* as the longest penalty shootout in history. Yet it ended 17-16 in favor of KK Palace.[123]

The question is why did they have to insist on a winner? The reason is that a winner must emerge in every true competition. Therefore, in every competitive sporting event, there can be only one

---

121 Guinness World Records, "Olympic Legends: Usain Bolt," August 5, 2016, https://www.guinnessworldrecords.com/news/2016/8/olympic-legends-usain-bolt-fastest-man-on-the-planet-438787.

122 Priya Singh, "Top 10 Fastest Runners," SportsUnfold.com, March 14, 2022, https://www.sportsunfold.com/top-10-fastest-runner-in-the-world-right-now/.

123 Guinness World Records, "Longest Penalty Shootout," accessed November 14, 2022, https://www.guinnessworldrecords.com/world-records/longest-penalty-shootout.

champion in each category, not two or three. The champion gets the gold medal. Others must learn to accept defeat.

In the category of the men's 100 m at the Los Angeles Olympics Games in 1932, an American athlete, Eddie Tolan, nicknamed the "Midnight Express," won the gold medal. However, Tolan and Metcalfe both finished the race at 10.38 seconds! The officials took hours to analyze the camera to decide who the winner was. "The films showed that Tolan and Metcalfe hit the finish line in a dead heat, but Tolan was declared the winner, because he had his entire torso past the line on the ground before Metcalfe."[124]

If such a thing as a win-win exists in competition, then Tolan and Metcalfe had the best case for it. They could have won the gold medal together, but that wasn't the case. So the winner was Tolan, not both. This is why Africans say, "There is always a winner, even in a monkey's beauty contest."

The same thing happens in politics. In 2022, the French presidential elections once again entered the second round. Just as it happened in 2017, it was between Emmanuel Macron and Marine Le Pen. In the end, on April 24, 2022, France elected just one president, Emmanuel Macron. So in every true competition, only one champion will emerge.

This point may not sit well with some, but the customers in your business are not your competitors. There is no competition when someone comes to your store to pick up the groceries, although bargaining may happen before paying. So winning or losing doesn't arise, and win-win is pointless.

Whenever there is competition, winning and losing are unavoidable. Therefore, leaders must learn the art of sportsmanship, also called

---

124 Wikipedia, "Eddie Tolan," last updated September 10, 2022, https://en.wikipedia.org/wiki/Eddie_Tolan.

fair play. Sportsmanship is a measure of someone's exemplary conduct in a competition. It means responding with maturity and grace in victory or defeat, regardless of the outcome.

At ISA, we always strive to win the tenders of our customers. Sometimes we fall short and lose. When we win, we celebrate. When we lose, we learn from our mistakes. We accept that winning and losing are facts of life.

Sportsmanship also means taking responsibility and not passing the blame to others—even in the face of an embarrassing defeat. On July 8, 2014, Brazil suffered a humiliating defeat in a FIFA World Cup semifinal match played inside the country at Mineirão stadium in Belo Horizonte. The match ended with a 7-1 score in favor of Germany. This was the worst defeat in history for Brazil. The Brazilian national coach, Luiz Felipe Scolari, took full responsibility. He said, "The catastrophic result can be shared with the whole group, but the choice and who decided the tactical lineup—I did. The person who is responsible is me."[125]

Leaders would do well to follow the example of this coach. Results will not always be in our favor. When this happens, we must own up to our mistakes and focus on ways we can improve. That is sportsmanship; it is the mindset of great coaches, and of course it should be the mentality of leaders too.

---

125   ESPN, "Scolari Takes Responsibility for Defeat," July 8, 2014, https://www.espn.com/ soccer/league-name/story/1940359/headline.

CHAPTER 11

PARENT

Every mother leaves her footprints.
—AFRICAN PROVERB

Parenting provides an exciting metaphor for leaders who seek to leave a legacy. It helps them prepare those who will take their organizations to greater heights long after their departure. This metaphor is very personal, and it involves a lot of emotions.

Daniel Goleman observed, "A view of human nature that ignores the power of emotions is sadly shortsighted."[126] Rather than ignore them, leaders should turn to the parenting playbook to ensure a happy ending when emotions such as fear, anger, happiness, and sadness take center stage.

EMOTIONAL INTELLIGENCE

Emotional intelligence involves managing your emotions and those of others to achieve successful outcomes. Many good parents under-

---

126   Daniel Goleman, *Emotional Intelligence: Why It Can Matter More Than IQ* (New York: Random House, September 27, 2005).

stand the importance of emotional intelligence. Yet sometimes, they respond poorly to a child who does not meet their expectations. On the extreme side, the frustrations of an abusive parent may degenerate into violence toward a child.

Fortunately, I am blessed to have parents who weren't perfect but were good examples. Also, being a father, I know that love is at the heart of positive parenting.

At home, loving parents may say to their kids, "I love you." Unfortunately, given the abuses in various workplaces, it is considered inappropriate to say those three words to a colleague. This verbal restriction does not imply that love cannot operate in the workplace. On the contrary, there are many ways we can show our genuine love and care for others in the workplace in a wholesome manner. How can you do this practically?

I have found a great example of practical, healthy love from an unlikely source. It is a 1976 highlife song by Nigerian-Cameroonian musician, the late Prince Nico Mbarga, titled "Sweet Mother." Growing up, I loved this song, which has become one of the most popular hits in Africa and has sold thirteen million copies.[127] Its original lyrics[128] are in Pidgin (the pseudo-English spoken widely in West Africa). My abridged translation is as follows:

Sweet Mother I Won't Forget You

For your suffering for me
When I cry my mother will carry me
She will say my child, please stop crying
When I want to sleep my mother will pet me

---

127   Wikipedia, "Sweet Mother," last updated January 29, 2022, https://en.wikipedia.org/wiki/Sweet_Mother.

128   Kamer Lyrics, "Prince Nico Mbarga," YouTube, February 23, 2014, 6:26, https://www.youtube.com/watch?v=XFqgZFdBJyU.

She will lay me down gently on the bed
She will cover me with a cloth and say sleep
Sleep, sleep my child
When I am hungry my mother will run around
She will find something for me to eat
When I am sick my mother will cry a lot
She will say instead of me let her be the one to die
She will plead with God, God help me, God help my child
If I don't sleep, my mother won't sleep
If I don't eat, my mother won't eat
She doesn't get tired
Sweet mother I won't forget your suffering for me

Sweet mother

For me, this is emotional intelligence in action. Good mothers practice it even when they have not read it in books. What Prince Nico said of his mother is also true of my mother, my wife, and many other caring mothers I know.

Amazingly, there's no single occurrence of the word "love" anywhere in the song. Yet it paints a vivid picture of motherly love that I recommend leaders emulate. Therefore, you do not need to go around and tell your coworkers, "I love you!" Instead, learn from a compassionate mother how to show love through your thoughtful actions that benefit people around you—especially when emotions are the focus.

In the words of the apostle John, "Dear children, let us not love with words or speech but with actions and in truth."[129] That is the

---

129   1 John 3:18.

key. John teaches us that we convey love best through our actions. However, even actions must have some boundaries.

BOUNDARIES

Please note that Prince Nico's song is an allegory of *early* childhood parenting. Your goal as a leader should never be to become a professional babysitter, where you go around treating your team members like babies. You want to help them become fully functioning adults who take the initiative independently. The last thing you need is a bunch of employees relying on you for everything. You want them to be emotionally independent and not constantly require nice words of encouragement to keep them motivated. Just as good parents nurture their kids to function independently, leaders should help their team members to think for themselves.

Growing up, my siblings and I had no doubt our mother loved us. Yet it was clear what type of behavior would get us into trouble. The rules weren't many, but they did exist. One of them was that we had to respond right away when she called us. In addition, our parents prohibited us from climbing trees due to numerous incidents where children fell and were injured. Then, one day, my elder sister, Lamen, broke both rules simultaneously!

She climbed the mango tree in our backyard and was about to pluck a fruit when she was surprised to hear our mother calling her. My sister faced an immediate dilemma. If she responded, she would reveal her whereabouts, providing incriminating evidence that she was breaking a rule. Whereas, if she didn't answer, she would be breaking another rule.

She tried to disguise her actual location. While quickly climbing down, she answered with her mouth half closed, making more of a humming sound than an intelligible response. As you may guess, my mom put the pieces together and punished my older sister for breaking both rules!

This illustration shows the need to set limits. When people work together, there must be guidelines on how to behave. You can learn from good parents how to establish healthy boundaries and enforce them when necessary. If you don't, you will end with anarchy that will destroy your organization. In *Boundaries: When to Say Yes, How to Say No*, Henry Cloud and John Townsend write, "Setting boundaries inevitably involves taking responsibility for your choices. You are the one who makes them. You are the one who must live with their consequences. And you are the one who may be keeping yourself from making the choices you could be happy with."[130]

> **Boundaries are guardrails that keep our leadership train on track as it moves steadily toward the destination, the intended outcome.**

Boundaries are guardrails that keep our leadership train on track as it moves steadily toward the destination, the intended outcome.

CONTINUITY

In a family, parents raise children until they reach maturity. Children, in turn, nurture their children. The process repeats indefinitely. Leaders can replicate this process of families and perpetuate their organizations as they continuously raise leaders to replace those who retire or resign.

In my late twenties, one of my uncles asked me about my plans concerning marriage. I gave a lengthy explanation of what I knew

---

130 Henry Cloud and John Townsend, *Boundaries: When To Say Yes, How to Say No* (Grand Rapids, MI: Zondervan, 2008), 45.

about marriage. He listened patiently. When I finished my lecture, he said, "Please go and get married!"

He wasn't alone in his opinion. Other extended family members also asked me until I married my lovely wife, Mhide. As I discovered, with countless newlyweds, the pressure never ceased and was only silent after we had children. This type of pressure can create unnecessary hardship for young people. Although I did not marry or have children due to these external voices, I still appreciate the belief behind such interests. It was his desire for me to keep the family lineage alive that my uncle began this conversation.

Leaders can use a similar mindset to create sustainable organizations. Long-term survival requires systems that allow experienced personnel to train juniors to maturity. This process is repeated consistently.

Leadership continuity thinking must saturate the organization to keep "the family lineage" alive. A study on CEO transitions in 2020 for S&P 500 firms by Stuart Spencer, a leadership consulting firm, is quite revealing: "Forty of the new CEOs—71 percent—were promoted from within the company, and 74 percent of those forty CEOs were identified as part of a planned succession. In 2019, 79 percent of new CEOs were internal successors, with 80 percent of internal promotions resulting from a planned succession."[131]

This means your company should have a steady flow of leaders for continuity. Succession plans for top management positions alone are not enough. Your business should remain very functional with any of its personnel's sudden resignation or anticipated retirement.

Sadly, some see their new colleagues as competitors. Rather than assisting, they would do anything to thwart their progress. This is very sad and the opposite of what responsible parents do. Sensible parents

---

131 SpencerStuart.com, "CEO Transitions 2020," April 2021, https://www.spencerstuart.com/research-and-insight/ceo-transitions-2020.

prepare their kids to go further than they have gone. Similarly, leaders should view their new colleagues as teammates who need support to grow. In my opinion, if you lose your job because you have trained a colleague, that organization is not worthy of your valuable service. You will be better off elsewhere.

At ISA, we have been working on leadership continuity for many years. The first time someone in our top management left, we had to reorganize our management team because we didn't have anyone sufficiently prepared to fill in. We learned from that experience and made changes such that planned or unplanned exits at any level no longer impact the effectiveness of our company.

In a nutshell, leadership continuity means the organization continues to function optimally, no matter who leaves, irrespective of the circumstances of their departure. Leaders will always want to leave something behind that is worth remembering when their time is over.

LEGACY

"How do you wish to be remembered?" That is the question often posed to parents and leaders when discussing the subject of legacy.

For someone like King David of ancient Israel, one may speculate that his answer to this question would most likely match what people later said about him. For many generations after his death, the Bible stated:

> For David had done what was right in the eyes of the Lord and had not failed to keep any of the Lord's commands all the days of his life—except in the case of Uriah the Hittite.[132]

---

132   1 Kings 15:5.

So David is portrayed positively, and his moral failure became an exception to his legacy. Unfortunately, not everyone enjoys that kind of balanced assessment.

The case of King Uzziah proved to be quite different. Among his outstanding achievements was the most advanced military technology invention of the era. 2 Chronicles 26:23 states:

> In Jerusalem he made devices invented for use on the towers and on the corner defenses so that soldiers could shoot arrows and hurl large stones from the walls. His fame spread far and wide, for he was greatly helped until he became powerful.

Unfortunately, what people remembered about him was far from flattering. They forgot all his good works, though he had been a good, powerful, and successful king. The Bible tells us that people remembered him as the king who "had leprosy."[133]

Therefore, when it comes to legacy, leaders can't impose their wishes on the memory of the people around or after them. So time spent on what you want people to remember you for is an exercise in futility. Does this mean leaders can't do anything about their legacy? Of course, they should. There's so much you can do to build your legacy. James Kouzes and Barry Posner wrote:

> The legacy you leave is the life you lead. We lead our lives daily. We leave our legacy daily. The people you see, the decisions you make, the actions you take—they are what tell your story.[134]

---

133 2 Chronicles 26:23.

134 James M. Kouzes and Barry Z. Posner, *A Leader's Legacy* (New York: Jossey-Bass, December 10, 2007).

In other words, your legacy is your footprints and fingerprints, not your future tombstone. As you live, wherever you "walk" or whomever you "touch," something remains to show you've been there. Therefore, you should ask yourself, "What am I doing with my life right now that could benefit others even when I am no longer around?"

Footprints remind me of someone I know and truly respect, Dr. James Zasha. He keeps meticulous records of his meditations. After twenty-four years, his meditations covered all sixty-six books of the Bible. He compiled them into a book titled *Footprints: Leaving Lasting Legacies*. Reading *Footprints* is inspiring. The book covers a wide "range of issues such as worldviews, politics, family, sex, ambition, government, justice, failure … and many other critical issues of life."[135]

This old saying is a confirmation: "Legacy is the responsibility of the living!" Therefore, what you are doing with your life right now for the benefit of others is your legacy.

---

135   James Zasha, *Footprints: Leaving Lasting Legacies* (June 30, 2021).

CHAPTER 12

JUDGE

If you close your eyes to facts, you will learn through accidents.
—AFRICAN PROVERB

Disclaimer: I am not a legal expert, so I am not qualified to provide legal advice. That said, this chapter is about using the metaphor of a judge for resolving conflicts within a team. Like the coach and parent, I consider this an internal metaphor when the leader's authority is not in doubt. It can also help you administer rewards and penalties fairly. Finally, it can serve as a framework for making ethical decisions. I'm not suggesting that every leader must become a legal expert. Instead, I am challenging you to learn from legal experts. In doing so, recognize the importance of knowing the laws and policies relevant to your leadership situation so you can confidently lead.

FRAMEWORK

It is critical to know the legal framework of where you live. Even a simple task, such as driving your car, requires you to be familiar with traffic regulations. Violations like driving through a red light may result in penalties, even if you claim ignorance. Oliver Wendell Holmes Jr. wrote, "Ignorance of the law is no excuse for breaking it."[136] Therefore, educating yourself on the relevant statutes and policies will help you avoid trouble.

A constitution contains the fundamental principles that govern a nation. Although it matters greatly, very few people take the time to read it. This is not surprising because even legal practitioners are not obliged to read it. Thomas Jipping, a senior legal fellow, wrote, "I took two courses in constitutional law in law school and was never required to read it [the Constitution]."[137]

I must admit that, until recently, I had never read the constitution of any country. Nevertheless, knowledge of the constitution of the country in which they live or operate is essential for leaders.

Besides their constitutions, leaders should also understand the laws applicable to their sector or jurisdiction. For instance, there are strict laws in nearly every country that govern financial institutions. If you are in that sector, no matter your role, you should know what the law says, so you do not mistakenly commit fraud. Similarly, you may have a breakthrough technology for drilling and extracting petroleum deposits. Yet without the proper license, you will be unable to utilize that technology.

Apart from the laws, the policies in your organization are also essential for making important decisions. It would be best to always rely on legal experts, but remember that the contracts you sign bear your signature. That means consent and full responsibility. You need

---

136 Oliver Wendell Holmes Jr., *The Common Law* (Mineola, NY: Dover Publications, July 22, 1991).

137 Thomas Jipping, "More Americans Need to Actually Read the Constitution," Heritage Foundation, November 1, 2019, https://www.heritage.org/the-constitution/commentary/more-americans-need-actually-read-the-constitution.

to understand their terms and recognize the general legal framework governing them.

Though it is essential to understand the law, in practice, only a few people think about it during the ordinary course of their work. Moreover, in these days of globalization, many organizations operate in multiple jurisdictions. Even for legal professionals, keeping track of all the laws, policies, and customs is a considerable challenge.

This raises the question, Are there any meaningful ways to meet all the different legal requirements effectively? Yes, I believe there are.

GOLDEN RULE

In 2011, the Angola parliament passed a new law to address the increase in domestic violence cases.[138] The authorities devised a simple billboard advertisement to raise awareness of the new law. It read, "Domestic violence is a crime." This simple summary of the domestic violence law of thirty-five articles served as a deterrent to citizens.

Similarly, you can find ways to simplify important corporate policies. Let us consider the example of the late Samuel Milton Jones, owner of Acme Sucker Rod Factory in Toledo, Ohio. He had one rule for his plant, and it said, "Therefore whatsoever, ye would that men should do unto you do ye even so unto them."[139]

This is known as the "Golden Rule." According to Wikimedia Commons, Mr. Jones "was known for his fair treatment of his employees, giving them a living wage and benefits unheard of at the

---

138 "Lei Contra A Violencia Domestica," lexlink.eu (ÓRGÃO OFICIAL DA REPÚBLICA DE ANGOLA, July 14, 2011), https://www.lexlink.eu/conteudo/angola/ia-serie/75270/lei-no-2511/14793/por-tipo-de-documentolegal.

139 Ohio Memory, "Golden Rule Sign," accessed November 14, 2022, https://www.ohiomemory.org/digital/collection/p16007coll33/id/107491DPLA.

time."[140] Mr. Jones, who died in 1904 at fifty-seven, didn't invent the Golden Rule. It came from the words of Jesus in Matthew 7:12 when he said, "So in everything, do to others what you would have them do to you, for this sums up the Law and the Prophets."[141]

Please note how Jesus ended it: "For this sums up the Law and the Prophets." Simply put, the Golden Rule is the essence of all the laws of Moses and the teachings of the prophets. It covers the most significant part of the Old Testament of the Bible!

Therefore, with the Golden Rule principle, you can lead impartially even with basic knowledge of the laws.

PRECEDENT

Another point from the legal profession that can be useful to leaders is the "legal precedent." "Precedents," as Credere Law explains, "are used when a court decision in an earlier case has similar facts and laws to a dispute currently before a court. Precedent will ordinarily govern the decision of a later similar case unless a party can show that it was wrongly decided or that it differed in some significant way."[142]

Another way of saying this is that your decision today becomes a standard for similar decisions in the future. So be careful when dealing with a matter for the first time because you are setting a precedent. The technology industry uses a similar term called "best practice." It is a suitable procedure that has worked well in the past and now serves as a helpful guide.

---

140 Ohio Memory, "Golden Rule Sign," accessed November 14, 2022, https://www. ohiomemory.org/digital/collection/p16007coll33/id/107491DPLA.

141 Matthew 7:12.

142 CredereLaw.com, "Legal Precedent Meaning," accessed November 14, 2022, https:// crederelaw.com/legal-precedent-meaning/.

Use precedent or best practice with caution. In the court system, the tension between the petitioner and the defendant in a judicial case ensures the correct use of precedents. As your operating environment may differ, be careful so you don't misapply a best practice. To guide against this error, I always ask, "Why?" And I reject answers such as "This is the way we have always done it."

TRUTH

The court system requires witnesses to take oaths before giving a judicial testimony. Though it differs from country to country, the text of a sworn testimony (oath or affirmation) usually contains a commitment to tell "the truth, the whole truth, and nothing but the truth."[143]

This statement raises several questions. Why is truth important? Why is lying wrong? Why should anyone be required to commit to telling the truth? James E. Rogan wrote, "If witnesses may lie with impunity for personal or political reasons, justice is no longer the product of the court system, and we descend into chaos."[144]

In other words, lies destroy the justice system and society. This is why perjury, which involves lying under oath, is considered a serious crime.

Leaders can learn from judges and put mechanisms in place, so truth remains the basis for constructive coexistence, even when team members have a conflict. However, simply taking an oath does not mean they cannot lie. After all, the judiciary has not been able to

---

143 Wikipedia, "Sworn Testimony," last updated July 29, 2022, https://en.wikipedia.org/wiki/Sworn_testimony.

144 *New York Times*, "An Obligation to Tell the Truth, the Whole Truth and Nothing but the Truth," January 15, 1999, https://archive.nytimes.com/www.nytimes.com/library/politics/011599impeach-rtext.html.

prevent lies, despite the solemn oath of each witness, just as James Stewart noted:

> We know the precise numbers for reported instances of rape, robbery, aggravated assault, burglary, larceny, and vehicle theft. No one keeps statistics for perjury and false statements—lies told under oath or to investigative and other agencies of the U.S. government—even though they are felonies punishable by up to five years in prison. There is simply too much of it, and too little is prosecuted to generate any meaningful statistics.[145]

If oaths don't help, what will help leaders avoid their organizations descending into the chaos caused by the scarcity of truth? It starts at the top. Every leader needs to make a personal commitment to the truth. Otherwise, your culture will suffer. For instance, if you ask your secretary to tell the caller that you are not in the office while you are sitting at your desk, then don't be surprised when she lies about why she came late to work the next day. She's simply speaking the language you have introduced to your company.

If you are not used to telling the truth, taking oaths won't change anything, no matter the prospect of perjury. For this reason, Jesus taught that you should "say only 'yes' if you mean 'yes,' and say only 'no' if you mean 'no.' If you must say more than 'yes' or 'no,' it is from the Evil One."[146]

A journalist for the Energy Year interviewed me some time ago. Present at the meeting was Claudia Abias. At that time, she was the head of the Quality Division of ISA. To my shame, I gave a dishonest answer to one of the questions! Neither Claudia nor the journalist

---

145　James B. Stewart, *Tangled Webs: How False Statements Are Undermining America From Martha Stewart to Bernie Madoff* (New York: Penguin, April 19, 2011).

146　Matthew 5:37 ICB.

could have known the truth easily, yet I knew in my heart that I had lied. Later that afternoon, I sent an email with an apology to both. I didn't want to hide my lie because of my pride. I don't want lies to become a habit in my life. Like they say in Botswana, "Ninety-nine lies may help you, but the hundredth lie will hurt you."

Therefore, humble yourself when you've realized you haven't lived up to the standard. Don't give excuses; own up and clean up before you move on. Without such remedial action, your lack of credibility will stand in the way of fair judgment.

FAIRNESS

Relevant statutes, precedent, and commitment to the truth are foundational to a fair judgment. Leaders can learn from good judges who do not rush to deliver a verdict no matter the pressure from others but instead follow the proper judicial process.

We once had an incident at our head office. Someone vandalized our sound system in the training room. Despite efforts, we could not find the person who committed the criminal act. We resisted the temptation of passing judgment without enough proof. Therefore, the only appropriate step was to improve security measures in our offices.

King Solomon of ancient Israel said, "The Lord hates two things. He hates it when the guilty are set free. He also hates it when those who aren't guilty are punished."[147] Therefore, if you cannot establish who committed an infraction, never punish someone strictly for "doing something." On the other hand, if the evidence points to an individual, follow the proper process. Start with the presumption of innocence,

---

147 Proverbs 17:15 NIRV.

which means that "the accused is innocent until proven guilty."[148] Then, take steps to check all the facts before arriving at a decision.

When your team has an interpersonal conflict, thinking like a judge will help you deal with it effectively. I grew up watching my dad serve as a "judge." He was chosen by the people and approved by the government as a community leader.

Don't give excuses; own up and clean up before you move on.

One of his duties was to ensure peace in the community in the most efficient way possible. Therefore, he and other elders would try to resolve conflicts peacefully without the police or the courts.

I remember one case that was brought to my dad. Out of jealousy, a man set the yams harvested by his neighbor on fire. Unfortunately for this perpetrator, there was overwhelming evidence that he was the culprit. My dad and the other elders visited the farms of both parties. They discovered that both had produced good harvests that year. The question was what would be a verdict that would be just and fair to both parties? My dad decided there would be a "yam swap"—one burnt yam of the offended for one good yam of the guilty party. The plaintiff accepted the proposed compensation. In the face of over-whelming evidence, the guilty party had no choice but to accept the verdict of the "court." So a team immediately went and swapped the yams, and the jealous man ended up with hundreds of burnt yams. Case closed.

As a leader, you do not have to be formally trained in law to judge fairly. My dad wasn't either. Nevertheless, you can learn from judges how to arrive at a fair judgment when you have authority, even

---

148 Steven H. Gifis, *Dictionary of Legal Terms: Definitions and Explanations for Non-Lawyers* (New York: Barron's Educational Services, November 1, 2015).

in a complicated interpersonal conflict. That said, you need to have a system for an appeal if a party is not satisfied with your verdict.

APPEAL

A classic example of this is the story of South African Olympic runner Oscar Pistorius. In the early morning of February 13, 2013, Pistorius shot and killed his girlfriend, Reeva Steenkamp, whom he allegedly mistook for an intruder.

As someone who had a disability and was still able to compete at the highest athletic levels, Pistorius's case generated worldwide attention. After a lengthy trial, Pistorius was not convicted of murder but was found guilty of culpable homicide and reckless endangerment with a firearm. He was sentenced to five years but was released on parole on October 19, 2015. However, the State appealed this conviction, and the Supreme Court of Appeal found Pistorius guilty of murder and sentenced him to six years imprisonment. The State appealed again and pleaded for a longer sentence. This time, the Supreme Court of Appeal handed down a fifteen-year sentence that he continues to serve.[149]

Why did the State continue to appeal the court's rulings, even though Pistorius was convicted? It was because the State considered the earlier verdicts too lenient. This shows that sometimes the judgment may not be acceptable to one party, which is why the right to appeal is an integral part of the judicial system. The appeal corrects inherent errors or oversights and keeps the court system credible.

As a leader, you should create a system where an aggrieved party can assert their right to appeal when needed. The right to appeal will enable you to correct your mistakes without external intervention.

---

149 Wikipedia, "Trial of Oscar Pistorius," last updated October 15, 2022, https://en.wikipedia.org/wiki/Trial_of_Oscar_Pistorius.

CHAPTER 13

PILOT

A chameleon that wants to survive from the burning bush
must abandon the majestic walk of its ancestors.

—AFRICAN PROVERB

The previous three chapters have examined metaphors that deal with the internal problems that leaders face, even when there is no doubt about their authority. The metaphors used were coach, parent, and judge. The following three chapters will aid in situations where a leader may not have adequate control or authority. Using pilot, soldier, and diplomat metaphors to address such external challenges may bring outstanding outcomes.

In this chapter, we will cover the pilot metaphor. You may recall that we humans, with two legs and two hands, shouldn't be able to fly. But for the envy of birds, we created airplanes that enable us to fly. Also, we keep pushing the boundaries from the Wright brothers' Kitty Hawk, or Wright Flyer, to Boeing's 787 Dreamliner. Consequently, hundreds of people with tons of goods can safely fly nonstop in one jumbo plane across continents. Moreover, through continuous improvement of engineering and procedures, now flying is safer than traveling by motorcycle, car, or train.

Are there things leaders can learn from pilots? Yes, absolutely. For instance, most airplane accidents happen during takeoffs and landings.[150] Similarly, more corporate bankruptcies occur during the start-up and decline stages of their life cycle.

By choosing to learn from pilots, leaders can improve the safety records of their ventures. Meaning, we can reduce corporate bank-ruptcies to the barest minimum if we decide to use the pilot metaphor. This chapter will teach critical lessons to prepare for and handle emer-gencies effectively. I am confident that doing so will make the "flying experience" pleasurable for everyone in your organization.

CERTIFICATION

To operate an aircraft, you need a license. The certification process for airline pilots is rigid to ensure the safety of passengers and crew members. Going through ATP Flight School takes most participants a minimum of seven months of pilot training and eighteen months of additional flight time to reach the hiring standards of fifteen hundred hours. During this two-year program, in addition to training, the candidate must pass written examinations such as the ATP and FAA.[151]

The results of these high standards make for a safe flying experi-ence. According to anxiety.com, we are "nineteen times safer in a plane

---

150   Amie Jane Leavitt, *Anatomy of a Plane Crash (Disasters)* (Mankato, MN: Capstone Press, July 1, 2010), 13.

151   HowExpert with Jeffrey Lawrence, "Pilot 101: How to Become a Pilot and Achieve Success in Your Aviation Career from A to Z," Hot Methods, March 14, 2019.

than in a car" and ten times safer flying than making a coast-to-coast trip by train.[152]

Flying has become the safest means of transportation because of the aviation industry's commitment to rigorous certification programs. However, other factors, such as the decades of continuous improvement of aircraft engineering and safety standards, have also contributed. Consequently, worldwide air travelers each year have increased for decades and reached an all-time high of 4.56 billion in 2019 before the COVID-19 disruption.[153]

Besides safety, certification programs bring other benefits, such as quality, performance, and sustainability. That is why most industries have them. Conversely, quality, safety, and performance suffer when standards are lacking.

In my many years of involvement at different levels of business management, I have observed that training makes a tremendous difference:

1. Certification boosts employees' confidence, which is very important.
2. There is a link between high productivity and good training.
3. Customers are generally more at peace with a certified professional than others.

Many organizations realize the importance of structured training and have leadership development programs that contribute immensely to achieving organizational goals.

---

152 "How Safe Is Commercial Flying?," Anxieties.com, accessed November 14, 2022, https://anxieties.com/86/flying-howsafe/.

153 World Bank, "Air Transport, Passengers Carried," accessed November 14, 2022, https://data.worldbank.org/indicator/IS.AIR.PSGR?end=2020&start=1970&view=chart.

BLACK BOX

Learning doesn't stop at certification. Pilots continue to learn valuable lessons from takeoff to landing on every flight. In addition, the aviation industry draws comprehensive lessons from each accident.

Air Canada Flight 797 is a good case study on how the airline industry applies lessons learned from accidents. In *Anatomy of a Plane Crash*, Amie Jane Leavitt wrote:

> In 1983, an electrical fire started behind the bathroom walls of Air Canada Flight 797. There was no smoke detector in the bathroom. The flight crew didn't find out about the fire until it was too late. No one died in the crash. Still, the smoke and fire ended up killing half the people on board.[154]

This disaster immediately prompted a series of changes:[155]

1. Bathrooms must have smoke detectors.
2. Aisle lighting must mark paths to the exit doors.
3. Firefighting training occurs for crew members.
4. Evacuation of all passengers occurs within ninety seconds.

Therefore, we can learn from pilots that applying lessons learned in accidents can prevent reoccurrence.

Early in my career, I worked as an on-site IT support engineer for an oil and gas customer. Whenever we had an incident, even a virus infection, on a computer, the managers insisted that we do a "root cause analysis." Once we understood the cause of the incident, we would discuss prevention measures followed by an action plan.

---

154 Amie Jane Leavitt, *Anatomy of a Plane Crash (Disasters)*.

155 Wikipedia, "Air Canada Flight 797," last updated October 25, 2022, https://en.wikipedia.org/wiki/Air_Canada_Flight_797.

I thought it was overkill back then, but in retrospect, the principle makes perfect sense. If you don't understand what caused the problem, then you can't be sure you can prevent it from happening again. Leaders can learn from the aviation industry how to best use lessons learned when things go wrong.

Christine Negroni, a well-known aviation journalist, noted:

> Investigations help illuminate how machines and humans fail, which in turn shows us how to prevent similar events. Because the aviation community has been so conscientious about this over the years, hurtling through the air at five hundred miles an hour and seven miles high is far less likely to kill you than almost any other type of transportation.[156]

Each aircraft has at least one orange-painted recorder, known as the *black box*. This important device records flight data and communication in the cockpit. It is more protected than anything else on the aircraft. By design, it sustains the least damage in the event of a crash. Investigators, therefore, use the information the black box records to analyze the cause of an accident, even if there are no survivors.

Every organization should ask whether they have a system that protects their critical data if a disaster occurs. There is a need to consider different scenarios and do everything possible to secure critical data should a disaster strike.

In the early 2000s, I served as the project manager for a disaster recovery project. In those days, it was primarily volumes of documentation that specified details of what everyone should do if a disaster happened. Since then, we have learned that reading one paragraph

---

156 Christine Negroni, *The Crash Detectives: Investigating the World's Most Mysterious Air Disasters* (New York: Penguin, September 27, 2016).

of instruction is already too much to expect of someone in a panic. Consequently, the focus has shifted to business continuity—that is, doing everything possible, so the business suffers minimal interruption even when a disaster occurs.

The main takeaway for every leader is that you and your organization must be prepared. In aviation terminology, you must keep your seat belt fastened even if the aircraft is cruising smoothly.

While preparedness is imperative for dealing with emergencies, excessive reliance on your plans can also be a problem. Jesus's parable of a rich man documented in Luke 12:16–21 dramatically illustrates this point:

> [16] And he told them this parable: The ground of a certain rich man yielded an abundant harvest. [17] He thought to himself, "What shall I do? I have no place to store my crops."

> [18] Then he said, "This is what I'll do. I will tear down my barns and build bigger ones, and there I will store my surplus grain. [19] And I'll say to myself, 'You have plenty of grain laid up for many years. Take life easy; eat, drink and be merry.'"

> [20] But God said to him, "You fool! This very night your life will be demanded from you. Then who will get what you have prepared for yourself?"

> [21] This is how it will be with whoever stores up things for themselves but is not rich toward God.

The tragic death of this rich man is unfortunate. It is equally shocking that God called him, "You fool!" Many Bible passages[157] teach us to be wise and prepare for the future. So what are leaders to learn from this parable? I would take it as a warning to us all. Making perfect plans for the frivolous while neglecting life's most important questions is not wise. Furthermore, the unexpected is inevitable in an increasingly volatile and complex world, and a disaster-proof plan is an illusion. That doesn't mean you shouldn't do anything at all about emergencies.

EMERGENCY LANDING

On the morning of January 15, 2009, Captain Chesley Sullenberger (known as Sully) piloted US Airways Flight 1549 out of New York City's LaGuardia Airport en route to Charlotte, North Carolina. Minutes after takeoff, the plane encountered a flock of birds that took out both aircraft engines. At first, Sully thought they might be able to land at a nearby airport, but he quickly realized he would have no option but to land the plane in the Hudson River.

The unexpected is inevitable in an increasingly volatile and complex world, and a disaster-proof plan is an illusion.

To everyone's astonishment, all 155 people on board survived the water landing. This incredible event became termed the "Miracle on the Hudson."

In an interview with Katie Couric, Captain Sullenberger described the difficulty involved with this emergency landing. "I needed to touch down with the wings exactly level," he shared. "I needed to touch down with the nose slightly up. I needed to touch down at a

---

157   Proverbs 6:6–8, 16:1–4, 31:10–31; Luke 14:28–32.

descent rate that was survivable. And I needed to touch down just above our minimum flying speed, but not below it. And I needed to make all these things happen simultaneously."[158]

Leaders can learn from Captain Sullenberger and other pilots that such maneuvering is not a matter of luck. It requires rigorous training, deliberate preparation, and adequate experience. Without these necessary steps, the outcome of emergencies may not be good.

That said, there are times when actions alone are not sufficient to save a leader in an emergency. An example is King Jehoshaphat of Judah. As 2 Chronicles 20 notes, a vast army from a coalition of hostile nations invaded his country. They advanced toward the capital city, Jerusalem. Jehoshaphat was afraid, as he was no match for their military power. Without any tangible way out, he turned to God in prayer. Suddenly, the coalition that came to destroy broke down and turned on each other. They killed themselves without Jehoshaphat engaging them in battle. That was miraculous!

Back in 1995, I was still in my early years as an on-site engineer on a client site in Warri, Southern Nigeria. I received good formal training. After nearly one year of on-the-job training, my supervisor felt I was ready to act as his temporary replacement. I was excited but also nervous, as it was my first time managing an operation of that size on my own.

During the first week, things went quite well. Unfortunately, the second week proved very difficult. My attempt to fix a minor system problem made the production system inaccessible at a critical hour. When this happened, I needed to collect my thoughts and think clearly. The bathroom was the only quiet place to escape the barrage of calls. Unfortunately, I was so nervous that the only thing I did in there was a simple prayer: "Lord, please help me."

---

158 Amie Jane Leavitt, *Anatomy of a Plane Crash (Disasters)*, 5.

After a few minutes, I stepped out of the restroom and returned to work. Then, I felt prompted to call my boss, who was away on vacation. In the midnineties, there were no mobile phones, and I knew there was only a slight chance he would answer. To my amazement, he did. He had just left his home and even locked the door behind him when he heard the phone ringing.

Through a brief conversation, he offered me a piece of advice that resolved the situation and got the system back up and running again. At that moment, I knew God had answered my prayer. I believe He took note of my feeble bathroom prayer and helped me in my moment of distress. Since that point, nearly three decades ago, I have had many other instances where the solution to a challenging situation came as an answer to my prayers. It's for this reason that I recommend prayer to all leaders.

I see prayer as communicating with God. It is as though the pilot is exchanging signals with the control tower during the entire flight. So when the pilot starts sending distress signals, there is no confusion about the message.

Prayer is a regular part of my daily routine. I constantly talk to God, knowing that He is in control. No emergency takes Him by surprise. Many leaders have relied on God since ancient times during crises that are well beyond their control. I am not suggesting that we fold our arms and expect God to compensate for our poor planning and execution. We must do our part even in emergencies.

In summary, the pilot metaphor reminds us of the need to prepare for all possible outcomes. Just as pilots undergo hours of training, you must train yourself and your teams for the unexpected. Then, when emergencies occur, you are ready to take charge.

CHAPTER 14

SOLDIER

It takes more courage to hold back than to fight back.

—TIV PROVERB

Few tragedies in life can compare to the horrors of war. Yet it is a constant in human history. Our world has only experienced twenty-six days of peace since the end of the second world war despite many treaties and other attempts at peace by global organizations such as the United Nations.[159] Armed conflicts are part of the history of every nation. That is why almost all countries have a defense department where soldiers work. The primary purpose is to protect the country from foreign invasion. Moreover, countries form alliances such as NATO to strengthen their defenses further.

Whether by sea, land, air, or cyberspace, soldiers are on the frontline of warfare, risking their lives in service for their country or cause. The rigorous training of soldiers exemplifies qualities such as discipline, courage, and loyalty. By observing them, leaders can learn how to handle tough situations confidently.

---

159 Institute for Scientific Cooperation, "Law and State," accessed November 14, 2022, https://epub.ub.uni-muenchen.de/10248/1/10248.pdf.

DISCIPLINE

Discipline is integral to all major military organizations. Even small disciplines, such as courtesy and cleanliness, seemingly unimportant to a soldier's ability to perform on the battlefield, are treated with the utmost scrutiny. In the words of US four-star Admiral William McRaven, "If you want to change the world, start off by making your bed."[160]

Soldiers need discipline because the stakes in battles are incredibly high. One poor choice can be the difference between life and death. A careless misfire can bring an entire unit into harm's way. Therefore, proper discipline saves lives and minimizes costly mistakes.

I have never served in the military. However, upon graduating from university, I participated in a one-year Nigerian government mandatory program, the *NYSC*.[161] The initial phase was a twenty-one-day orientation program that was paramilitary training led by a group of soldiers. That is the closest I have ever gotten to being a soldier. It left an indelible mark on me. I still remember there was no room for lateness. Everything had to be done on time and in a precise manner. It took many days of practice, but eventually all the corps members in the camp marched together in unison in the local parade.

Sometimes, discipline means restraining yourself from lashing out against others, even when you feel their attack on you is very unjust. In *8 Lessons in Military Leadership for Entrepreneurs*, Robert Kiyosaki explained how he handled an incident in 1973 involving his team of marines as they returned from their tour in Vietnam.

As they neared a group of antiwar protesters, Robert reminded his fellow marines of why they fought. "We fight for freedom and the

---

160 Admiral William H. McRaven, *Make Your Bed: Little Things That Can Change Your Life ... and Maybe the World* (New York: Grand Central Publishing, April 4, 2017).

161 "National Youth Service Corps," Wikipedia (Wikimedia Foundation, December 9, 2022), https://en.wikipedia.org/wiki/National_Youth_Service_Corps.

rights of all people, not for select groups of people," he told them. Robert explained what followed: "In silence, [the marines] shouldered their bags, turned, and walked through the protesters, with their heads held high, their backs straight, their eyes focused … saying nothing as spit, eggs, and verbal abuse were hurled at them."[162]

It takes great discipline, anchored in a clear sense of purpose, to hold yourself back when you feel an attack on you is unfair. All leaders must understand this.

Understanding my purpose helped me in the early 90s when Africans started migrating to Europe and North America in droves. There were solid reasons for this emigration. With the rise in social, political, and economic issues, leaving for the promise of a better life elsewhere was very understandable. Rather than follow the multitude, my good friend, Ogbo Awoke Ogbo, and I decided to seek God's guidance through a period of fasting and prayer. In the process, we grew convinced that we had a contribution to make in Africa, even though we were uncertain what this should be. A glimpse of my purpose instilled in me the discipline to stay in Africa rather than join the bandwagon. To this day, I have no regrets. I have remained in Africa, trying to make that contribution.

Therefore, discipline could also mean having a sense of purpose and relentlessly focusing on it until you see the result—and that takes courage.

COURAGE

That brings us to the second important quality of a soldier—courage. Like discipline, courage requires a sense of purpose. When Joshua

---

162   Robert T. Kiyosaki, *8 Lessons in Military Leadership for Entrepreneurs* (Scottsdale, AZ: Plata Publishing, May 12, 2015), 32.

took over the leadership of the nation of Israel, he was told on several occasions to be strong and courageous. The objective was to bring people to inherit the land God promised their ancestors.[163]

Courage does not eliminate fear. Instead, it gives us the resolve to confront our fears and face difficult situations. There are examples of people who have shown great courage yet were not soldiers. For example, on June 10, 2022, a Nigerian truck driver, Ejiro Otarigho, exhibited great bravery when he drove a burning tanker out of town to save the lives of others. His apprentice noticed and informed him of the fire at the back of the tanker. Ejiro immediately slowed the truck down and encouraged

Consistent quality attracts loyalty, which is the aspiration of most corporate executives.

his assistant to jump out. He then kept driving the burning tanker for more than twenty minutes out of town, all the way to the nearby river. In an interview after the incident, he said, "I have to be honest with you. I was scared, but I don't know what gave me so much courage. I was not seeing the danger; I was looking at the damage that would happen if I cowered and jumped off the tanker. Thousands of people would have died."[164]

Ejiro's concern for others outweighed his desire to preserve his life. People like him serve as a model for leaders. They remind us that we can make good, selfless, and courageous decisions. We can act with wisdom and bravery for the good of others.

Unfortunately, some leaders view themselves as generals who lead their troops into battle each day to attack anyone they consider a threat.

---

163 Deuteronomy 31:6, 7, 23; Joshua 1:6–9, 18.

164 Godfrey George and Temitope Adetunji, "I Want Another Tanker, Not National Honour—Delta Man Who Drove Burning Fuel Truck to Avert Tragedy," PunchNG.com, June 19, 2022, https://punchng.com/i-want-another-tanker-not-national-honour-delta-man-who-drove-burning-fuel-truck-to-avert-tragedy/.

This behavior is detrimental and causes many internal conflicts (civil wars). It may also lead to undesirable outcomes such as price wars.

In a price war, the territory to be won is the customer. The weapon is the price, and the competition is the enemy. Price wars usually don't end well for all sides involved. Aksay Rao published an article in the *Harvard Business Review*. He stated:

> Price wars can create economically devastating and psychologically debilitating situations that take an extraordinary toll on an individual, a company, and industry profitability. No matter who wins, the combatants all seem to end up worse off than before they joined the battle.[165]

Price is not the only reason why customers buy. If this were the case, Ferrari wouldn't sell cars, and no one would buy an iPhone. There are myriads of cheaper alternatives to these products. So rather than engage in a price war, find ways to distinguish your company in product quality and customer service. Consistent quality attracts loyalty, which is the aspiration of most corporate executives.

LOYALTY

That brings us to the last of our three primary characteristics of a soldier—loyalty. In *Men Against Fire*, Brigadier General Marshall wrote, "Loyalty is the big thing, the greatest battle asset of all."[166]

---

165 Akshay R. Rao, Mark E. Bergen, and Scott Davis, "How to Fight a Price War," *Harvard Business Review*, March–April 2000, https://hbr.org/2000/03/how-to-fight-a-price-war.

166 S. L. A. "Slam" Marshall, *Men Against Fire: The Problem of Battle Command* (OK: University of Oklahoma Press, September 15, 2000).

The disloyal soldiers who should be protecting may be the ones who cause someone's death. Therefore, strength is dreadful in the absence of loyalty, and courage becomes a threat.

Loyalty is imperative for businesses as well. Loyal employees who feel a strong sense of belonging provide companies with the stability they seek. These are the ones who are less likely to quit. Over time, they contribute significantly to the company's growth. Leaders who want the commitment of such employees must prove themselves worthy of trust.

Also, many companies create loyalty programs for their customers. One example is the frequent flyer program offered by virtually all airlines. Over the years, I have signed up as a frequent flyer on some airlines. I use the accumulated miles whenever possible to upgrade my ticket to a higher class. However, my loyalty only goes so far. My preference will always be the airline that provides the best service. So if you want customer loyalty, please make sure you offer superior quality of service.

Loyalty does not mean we never speak our minds and just go along with every poor decision a leader above us makes. To avoid blind loyalty, General Colin Powell offered this qualification:

> When we are debating an issue, loyalty means giving me your honest opinion, whether you think I'll like it or not. Disagreement, at this stage, stimulates me. But once a decision has been made, the debate ends. From that point on, loyalty means executing the decision as if it were your own.[167]

---

167 Colin L. Powell and Joseph E. Persico, *My American Journey* (New York: Random House, September 1995), 284.

Let me reiterate that loyalty is multidirectional and is not just bottom-up. Captain Sir Basil Liddell Hart said:

> We learn from history that those who are disloyal to their own superiors are most prone to preach loyalty to their subordinates. Loyalty is a noble quality, so long as it is not blind and does not exclude the higher loyalty to truth and decency.[168]

In summary, the soldier metaphor gives the leader the discipline and courage to make good decisions in tough situations while also being loyal.

---

168 *The Greenhill Dictionary of Military Quotations* (London: Greenhill Books, January 1, 2006), 268.

CHAPTER 15

DIPLOMAT

Just because the lizard nods its head does not mean it is in agreement.

—AFRICAN PROVERB

Despite being the last of our leadership metaphors, this is the one I now consider most important. Regrettably, my upbringing hindered me from appreciating this metaphor sooner.

Born of the Tiv tribe in Benue State, Nigeria, I grew up in a setting where "real men" were supposed to be strong, bold, and direct. Uncle Moses Chigh said, "We sometimes derive pleasure in punishing people with the truth."[169] Our traditional black-and-white (zebralike) attire called "A'nger u Tiv" reveals our fundamental outlook on life. It is either day or night, good or bad, yes or no, and life or death. There is no middle ground. I lived that way until 2007 when I compiled all the leadership metaphors into one document.

When I came to the diplomat metaphor, its importance hit me like lightning. I remembered many painful experiences I could have avoided if I had been tactful. I realized that sensitive situations require

---

169 Moses Chigh, personal communication, October 26, 2012.

diplomacy, although truth remains an unshakable foundation. Since then, I have developed a healthy respect for diplomats. I pay particular attention to ambassadors and other professional diplomats. Honestly, I don't entirely agree with all their decisions. However, I have gained valuable insights by observing them handle sensitive situations. In addition, the autobiographies of Kofi Annan and Ban Ki-moon have been very helpful.

Leaders can apply lessons learned from diplomats to give and receive feedback positively. Through diplomacy, we can reconcile broken relationships and resolve delicate issues. That said, diplomacy is hard work. Sometimes it takes years of arduous negotiations before the parties in conflict shake hands in agreement. Furthermore, diplomats often get positive results when hope seems lost, and disaster looms.

NEGOTIATION

One of the essential points you can learn from diplomats is how to negotiate for good outcomes in different situations. The negotiated settlement of the Bakassi conflict is a case to consider.

Bakassi is a 665 km^2 peninsula situated at the extreme eastern end of the Gulf of Guinea, with a population of about three hundred thousand. Nigeria and Cameroon came to the verge of war several times over contradictory claims that both had in this area with large oil and gas reserves. Africans always question the legitimacy of colonialism. Therefore, it is fascinating that both countries had no qualms about citing colonial-era agreements between European countries as evidence of their ownership of Bakassi.[170]

---

170 Wikipedia, "Bakassi," last updated November 3, 2022, https://en.wikipedia.org/wiki/Bakassi.

That notwithstanding, the International Court of Justice delivered its judgment on October 10, 2002, that Bakassi belongs to Cameroon. However, implementing the ruling wasn't that simple. Most Bakassians are Nigerians, and the judgment never required them to move or change their nationality! Therefore, a complex negotiation ensued, taking almost four years. Finally, on June 12, 2006, Nigeria and Cameroon signed a treaty known as the Greentree Agreement. Kofi Annan, UN secretary-general at the time, made the following opening statement at the event:

> It gives me great pleasure to welcome all of you today. The signing ceremony which has brought us together crowns a remarkable experiment in conflict prevention by Cameroon and Nigeria. Many individuals have worked tirelessly to realize today's Agreement. I am particularly proud of the UN's role in supporting from the beginning this innovative process. But we are here, first and foremost, thanks to the vision of Presidents Biya and Obasanjo, two leaders of uncommon courage and foresight. Nearly four years ago, in an inspiring example—that I hope will be emulated by others—of African leaders coming together to resolve differences peacefully, they resolved to settle their countries' border dispute in accordance with international law.[171]

Fortunately, the negotiations came to a successful conclusion in this case. There was no war, and innocent lives didn't have to die. Where such talks have failed, the outcomes were bloody wars, such as in Yugoslavia, Iraq, Somalia, Angola, Rwanda, and the Israeli-Palestine

---

171   United Nations, "Secretary-General's Statement on Bakassi Peninsula," June 12, 2006, https://www.un.org/sg/en/content/sg/statement/2006-06-12/secretary-generals-statement-bakassi-peninsula.

conflict. Each conflict resulted in numerous casualties, incalculable suffering, and wanton destruction of properties.

In the case of Bakassi, apart from the UN and the two countries in conflict, the United States, Britain, France, and Germany were there as witnesses. Britain and France have recent colonial ties to Nigeria and Cameroon, so their presence was no surprise. Germany was a signatory to some of the agreements cited in the case. The United States was present, most likely due to economic interest. The negotiators knew that the most important stakeholders had to be present if the deal would remain intact. Therefore, engage all relevant stakeholders if you want a binding agreement.

Successful negotiation also saved my company. Several years ago, two shareholders decided to sell off all their shares. Due to legal hurdles, we couldn't do a buyback. Curiously, one of our competitors showed interest, but I suspected malicious intent. I then decided to step in to do the acquisition myself. However, the value they wanted was higher than what I could afford. Meanwhile, some staff who knew what was happening started to worry about the company's future.

I repeatedly read *The Negotiation Genius*, by Professor Deepak Malhotra, to prepare myself for the negotiation. It gave me a good understanding of the process that I followed. I also learned that maintaining a good relationship with all the stakeholders well past the deal was very important. Meanwhile, I took a friend's advice and structured appropriate payment terms instead of a bank loan. With that, I reached a deal with the two shareholders and saved the company.

Your ability to negotiate will help even in your prayers to God. In Exodus chapters 32–34, Moses demonstrated excellent negotiation skills in his prayers to save his people. After more than four hundred years in Egypt, a series of supernatural interventions culminated in the people of Israel, then enslaved people, leaving Egypt. While in the desert camping at Mount Sinai, God gave them laws to follow. The first of them was that they must not worship other gods (Exodus 20:3). It was a unanimous vote by the people to ratify the agreement. As Exodus 24:3 notes, "When Moses went and told the people all the Lord's words and laws, they responded with one voice, 'Everything the Lord has said we will do.'"

Moses temporarily handed over the leadership of the people to Aaron. He went to the mountain to collect the copies of the agreement that were divinely inscribed (Exodus 24:14–18). After a few weeks of Moses's absence, the people abandoned the agreement. Without hesitation, Aaron took a special collection of gold. He molded a statue of a young bull, also known as the golden calf. They worshipped it as their god and had wild parties.

Tragically, the people had "become corrupt" (Exodus 32:7), and God would destroy them. Seeing how events had shifted from bad to worse, Moses began negotiating with God on behalf of the people still enjoying their revelries. Acknowledging they had greatly sinned, Moses premised his negotiations on God's earlier agreements with their ancestors, which hadn't expired. He also pleaded for God's compassion and mercy. Moses persisted in his negotiation until God agreed. Thus, they had a new agreement (Exodus 34:10–28). And the people continued their journey to their new homeland.

Moses's ability to negotiate in prayer saved his people's lives. I, therefore, encourage leaders to emulate his excellent example when presenting petitions to God. They should also use diplomacy when giving feedback to others.

FEEDBACK

In speaking our minds, especially when giving feedback, we sometimes neglect the feelings of the person on the receiving end. But a good diplomat always pays attention to others' feelings and interests. Lying is not a virtue by any means, but the way you tell the truth is crucial. Truth spoken harshly can make your remarks unpleasant. "Speaking the truth in love"[172] can heal and create a harmonious relationship.

I consider it an essential aspect of my duties to review the performance of those who work with me periodically. I remember one occasion when a staff member ended an appraisal session abruptly.

If you want accurate information on how you are doing, focus on the core message.

Though I had sincerely focused on being truthful, my insensitive approach ruined my well-intentioned feedback. So, when giving feedback, please ensure you are not simply speaking your mind but following the counsel of Apostle Paul. He said in Ephesians 4:29, "Do not let any unwholesome talk come out of your mouths, but only what is helpful for building others up according to their needs, that it may benefit those who listen." In other words, state your feedback so that even a short-tempered person may still benefit from it.

On the other hand, don't give someone conditions they must follow to provide you with feedback. If you want accurate information on how you are doing, focus on the core message. Insisting on "constructive criticism" may deprive you of a critical perspective you genuinely need. I often solicit feedback from colleagues, mentors, friends, partners, my wife, and children. I encourage every leader to do the same.

---

172 Ephesians 4:15.

When you ask for feedback, please humble yourself and listen carefully, even if you may not like what you hear. Similarly, it is very prudent for you to receive unsolicited feedback with thankfulness. Proverbs 9:8 says, "Do not rebuke mockers or they will hate you; rebuke the wise and they will love you."

Even the worst of criticisms has benefits! In 1997, a few months after, I became a supervisor. I went to a client site with some of my team members for a planned intervention. Unfortunately, the client didn't show up even after we waited for an hour. Without any means to contact him, I left a note at the reception to call us when he arrived. We then went back to our office, which wasn't far away.

My colleague, a supervisor in another department, wondered why we returned so early. After I explained, he said that my predecessor had never had such issues. My poor planning was the problem. I was infuriated. Then I replied that I, too, preferred to work with his predecessor, but there was no use reminding him about it. Moving closer and pointing my finger to his face, I warned him: "Never compare me to anyone again. Do you understand?" I then stormed out.

Later that evening, I recounted the encounter to my senior friend, Mr. Udobong Idemetor, expecting him to congratulate me for my great courage. However, his response was remarkably different! He said, "A few years from now, you will laugh off a similar situation."[173] This means he saw that my handling of the provocation was immature, inappropriate, and excessive.

Fast-forward to more than a decade later. While serving on the leadership council of my local church, I presented its annual budget. After which, an attendee launched a tirade of verbal attacks on me. I listened carefully, but I didn't understand his point. In the end, the general assembly approved the budget by near-unanimous votes.

---

173 Udobong Idemetor, personal communication, 1997.

This angered him more. He then sent a long email with all sorts of accusations. I considered everything he said and sought counsel from mentors and friends. In the end, what I could have done differently was elusive. Though disappointed, I didn't feel any internal pressure to fight back.

How did the two incidents differ apart from the passage of time? In the first one, I had unwittingly considered the criticism an act of "war," and I fought back like a "soldier" with my verbal rockets to put the "enemy" in his place! In the second one, my focus was on learning. Nevertheless, it shouldn't take anyone years to learn how to handle criticism properly. Thinking like a diplomat, remembering the worst of all criticisms has at least one benefit, is what you need. So what could this minimum benefit be?

A maturity test! Bulus Bossan, a member of the International Executive Team of the Navigators, once said:

> There are people that God sends your way to help you grow, and there are some that are sent to test if truly you are growing. Both categories are necessarily good for you.[174]

So, when next you are criticized, don't forget that at least it is a maturity test. I hope you pass without the need for blood pressure medication!

Once again, as a leader, you shouldn't insist on "constructive criticism" when receiving feedback. However, when you give feedback, you should do so with tact.

---

174   Bulus Bossan, personal communication, April 2015.

TACT

Diplomats always consider the feelings and interests of others. Therefore, honest diplomats use praise and not flattery in acknowledging the efforts and achievements of others. To understand the difference between praise and flattery, let us look at Matthew 22:15–22, where the Pharisees and the Herodians (usually enemies) came to Jesus with a foolproof plan to trap him:

> Then the Pharisees went out and laid plans to trap him in his words. [16] They sent their disciples to him along with the Herodians. "Teacher," they said, "we know that you are a man of integrity and that you teach the way of God in accordance with the truth. You aren't swayed by others because you pay no attention to who they are. [17] Tell us then, what is your opinion? Is it right to pay the imperial tax to Caesar or not?" [18] But Jesus, knowing their evil intent, said, "You hypocrites, why are you trying to trap me? [19] Show me the coin used for paying the tax." They brought him a denarius, [20] and he asked them, "Whose image is this? And whose inscription?"
>
> [21] "Caesar's," they replied. Then he said to them, "So give back to Caesar what is Caesar's, and to God what is God's." [22] When they heard this, they were amazed. So they left him and went away.

Ordinarily, the "praise" in verse 16 is truthful. Jesus's integrity, humility, and teachings deserve many compliments. It is what many of his followers also said about him. The next verse reveals the deadly setup: "Tell us then, what is your opinion? Is it right to pay the imperial tax to Caesar or not?"

Please note that these two groups were at opposite ends regarding imperial tax. The Pharisees were anti-imperial tax. The Herodians were proimperial tax. In choosing a closed-ended question, they hoped that Jesus would fall into their trap either way.

Thus, I define flattery as praise followed by a trap. Jesus responded with a question of his own: "Why are you trying to trap me?" Despite knowing their evil intentions, Jesus showed no anger because sensitive situations require tact, not anger. Instead, he got the audience involved. The people responded that the coin used to pay imperial tax had Caesar's portrait and inscription. Finally, he said, "Give to Caesar what is Caesar's and to God what is God's." His point was so clear that they dispersed, wondering how their well-crafted plan failed miserably in the face of the superior wisdom and tact of the Master Diplomat.

Therefore, leaders should learn to respond to sensitive situations with tact instead of fury and wisdom instead of flattery.

HOT MIC

Certain sensitive situations require silence rather than words. Those who are married understand there are times when your spouse needs your ears more than your mouth. In such moments, even nice words may be problematic. Therefore, you must learn to listen with humility. That doesn't mean words are not important.

Times come when we must speak. One of those moments for Mr. Gordon Brown, the former British prime minister, was an encounter with Mrs. Gillian Duffy during his campaign in 2010. The exchange ended on a friendly note with a warm handshake. Then, Duffy went away, saying, "He is such a nice person." As he got into the car, Brown complained to his assistants: "That was a disaster—they should never have put me with that woman … she was just a bigoted woman." Unfortunately, the conversation wasn't private, as he still had his microphone on! It didn't take long before his comments were all over the news.[175]

What happened to Gordon Brown is known as "hot mic"—an error in which the microphone remains on without the speaker realizing it.[176] It causes embarrassment and can sometimes lead to serious reactions. For example, during a soundcheck, former US president Reagan made an infamous joke: "We begin bombing in five minutes." As a result, the Soviets put their forces on high alert![177] Some even lost their jobs because of such a blunder. Therefore, a popular precaution is, "Always assume the microphone is on." Some call this safeguard "the golden rule of politics." This safeguard is much needed these days, as someone with a smartphone can easily record your conversation and use it against you. Indeed, you can still speak intimately with your spouse in your bedroom or discuss a confidential business strategy in your company's boardroom. Of course, it is undesirable and awkward when such secrets come into the open.

However, as in Gordon Brown's case, what creates serious problems is the inconsistency between private and public statements. So, yes, it is the discrepancy that is very problematic for leaders. Therefore, what kind of safeguard will be effective? When it comes to words, your mouth is simply an outlet. That is why we need to search deep to discover their source. Jesus said in Luke 6:45, "A good man brings good things out of the good stored up in his heart, and an evil

---

175 Sky News, "Gordon Brown Calls Labour Supporter a 'Bigoted Woman,'" YouTube, April 28, 2010, https://www.youtube.com/watch?v=yEReCN9gO14.

176 Wikipedia, "Hot Mic," last updated November 10, 2022, https://en.wikipedia.org/wiki/Hot_mic.

177 BBCNews.com, "Five 'Hot Mic' Moments That Got Leaders in Trouble," December 4, 2019, https://www.bbc.com/news/world-50662928.

man brings evil things out of the evil stored up in his heart. For the mouth speaks what the heart is full of."

That means the heart is the actual source! What, then, should we do about it? Proverbs 4:23 teaches, "Above all else, guard your heart, for everything you do flows from it." That is undoubtedly the solution to the hot mic problem. With pure thoughts, private conversations will validate what you say publicly. Additionally, your social media accounts will have no inappropriate images. Hackers will find nothing incriminating in your emails, and you will have no fear of Wikileaks.

In conclusion, the diplomat metaphor provides critical tactical skills in dealing with sensitive situations. It will help you structure deals acceptable to the negotiating parties while maintaining your integrity. It also enables you to give feedback without irritating your audience.

As you work in a group of any size or kind, diplomacy will help you synergize seamlessly. Likewise, this metaphor will guide you to a terrific takeoff when starting in a new position or environment. In the remaining chapters, we shall see how you can use these metaphors practically and seamlessly as a leader.

PART IV

SEAMLESS

CHAPTER 16

SYNERGIZE

One finger cannot wash the whole face.

—AFRICAN PROVERB

The metaphors we covered in the earlier chapters have helped me appreciate my strengths and weaknesses and those of others around me. Some come naturally to me. However, there are others that I struggle to implement. For example, from a strategic standpoint, I've come to understand that I'm good at architect and engineer metaphors, but I'm not a good builder. From a tactical perspective, I use coach and parent metaphors but struggle as a diplomat.

In an era of interconnectivity, cooperation is no longer by choice but a necessity.

After surveying participants from my leadership seminars over the past few years, I've discovered I am not alone. Everyone has their areas of strength and weakness. Despite these limitations, many leaders I know have done great things by joining with others within and outside their organizations.

It's a good thing they have made this decision. In an era of inter-connectivity, cooperation is no longer by choice but a necessity. We need to join with others to create synergy to be successful. That said, working with others has its share of challenges. Fortunately, essential elements such as adaptability, collaboration, and humility can help the leader excel despite obstacles.

ADAPTABILITY

Adaptability is a team trait that emerges when team members alter their roles to address a challenge. It requires team members to be flexible and creative. In addition, it needs a good level of shared understanding. That explains why group members who have worked together for long periods tend to be more adaptable.

During my time at ISA, I've seen colleagues willingly take on leadership challenges according to their strengths and irrespective of their job titles. That flexibility of our people is significant to our survival as a company. One recent incident in the company can attest to my point. In a meeting with our HR manager, Sandra Monteiro, a staff member experienced an emotional frenzy. Rather than handle this situation alone, Sandra sought the help of the head of finance, Mabanza Francisco. Mabanza was able to put things under control with the support of an administration staff member, Hélio Manuel. It was a brilliant demonstration of adaptability. No one cared about their job titles but did what was needed to pass the emotionally charged test.

There is nothing new about adaptability in leadership. It's a concept that leaders like Moses applied thousands of years ago. After the Israelites departed from Egypt, while they remained in the wilderness, the Amalekites made a surprise attack on the worn-out, tired, and lagging community members. To defend themselves, the leaders of this mobile community had to adapt their roles quickly.

Moses delegated Joshua to lead some of their men to the front of the battle. He went up to the nearby hillside with two of his assistants, Aaron and Hur, to pray. While on top of the hill, they observed a very unusual phenomenon. When Moses lifted his arms, the Israelites advanced. When he lowered them, the Amalekites gained the upper hand. As you might imagine, past the age of eighty, it was not an easy task to keep his hands up for hours.

Nevertheless, the survival of the whole nation depended on Moses's tired hands remaining in the air! Realizing this, Aaron and Hur had him sit on a stone while they held up his hands till evening. Thus, Joshua succeeded in fending off the ruthless attackers! Delegated or volunteered, each person worked hard for the community's survival.

Let me put it this way: a leader is not Superman or Wonder Woman. You don't need to have the ability to deal with every situation on your own. Also, job titles are of no importance when stakes are high, as demonstrated by Aaron, Hur, and Mabanza. Instead, everyone must take up complimentary roles to deal with the problem. That is what I call adaptability. An organization that consistently works this way can survive turbulent times.

No matter how endowed your team may be, there will be moments when you will not have at hand sufficient capabilities to get the outcome you desire. If you have resources elsewhere in the organization, internal transfers may likely help. Also, recruitment is a good way of bringing into your company the missing know-how. King Solomon did that when he wanted to build a large temple in ancient Jerusalem but didn't have anyone in his country with sufficient skills to create its furnishings. So he hired Huram from Tyre, a skilled craftsman in bronze who helped complete the magnificent project.[178]

There are people you need who you will not be able to hire. Yet without their help, some opportunities will be lost. In this case, collaboration will be your best option.

COLLABORATION

Working with others outside your realm of authority requires collaboration. As Chris McGoff noted in his book *The Primes*:

> Many of the problems we face cannot be solved within the confines of a single corporate or organizational entity. Problem-solving groups increasingly are coalitions of the willing and loose confederations of people drawn together from various loyalties, perspectives, and intentions.[179]

Leading a group without formal authority presents a different kind of challenge. This is what I see as Tiago's situation. Tiago is the coordinator of the small neighborhood community where I live. Each house has its owner, though we share common facilities such as the park, electricity, and water supply. That means Tiago must always find creative ways to get the homeowners to collaborate; otherwise, projects get stalled.

Tiago is not alone. Most leaders know that getting others to do things willingly is not always easy. For example, former US president Harry Truman once grumbled, "I sit here all day trying to persuade

---

178   1 Kings 7.

179   Chris McGoff, *The Primes: How Any Group Can Solve Any Problem* (New York: Wiley, April 3, 2012).

people to do things they ought to have sense enough to do without my persuading them ... That's all the powers of the president amount to."[180]

Consequently, one may erroneously want to opt for dictatorship to bypass bureaucracy and get quick results. Those who have firsthand experience warn against this. In the wake of the Arab Spring, as many well-established dictators crumbled in the region, Wadah Khanfar, director general of Al Jazeera, observed, "Good leaders need to build consensus. It would be easier to be a dictator. But it doesn't work."[181]

Building consensus doesn't require everyone to agree. Instead, it means there are enough people in agreement to move forward with an idea. That requires patience and persuasion skills that leaders can learn from diplomats.

Please note that collaboration is not limited to leadership in the neighborhood community. The internet and social media redefine how we communicate, buy, travel, think, live, and lead. The internet has unveiled a powerful dimension of collaboration known as crowdsourcing.

CROWDSOURCING

Crowdsourcing means getting many people (usually internet users from all over the world) to contribute their skills, thoughts, contacts, and money to a cause or project.

One such example is Wikipedia, an online multilingual encyclopedia. It's considered the most-read reference work in history. Jimmy Wales and Larry Sanger cofounded it in 2001, and the Wikimedia Foundation manages it. At the time of this writing, Wikipedia has

---

180   Richard E. Neustadt, *Presidential Power and the Modern Presidents: The Politics of Leadership from Roosevelt to Reagan* (New York: Free Press, March 1, 1991).

181   *Portfolio Magazine*, issue 69, September 2011.

an active community of 113,963 volunteers in an open collaboration who write 586 new articles a day. Moreover, it has 44 million registered users, some of whom have contributed to more than 56 million pages.[182] By contrast, its notable rival, Encyclopedia Britannica, has existed for two and a half centuries yet has published less than 0.5 percent of Wikipedia articles.[183]

Just because anyone can edit its pages, you may think that Wikipedia should rank very low on accuracy. On the contrary, many studies have found that Wikipedia has a similar accuracy rating to other encyclopedias.[184] Moreover, social computing researcher Professor Amy Bruckman considers Wikipedia more accurate than its peers in some categories. She wrote:

> "A journal article goes through the review process once, and then is frozen. If new information emerges to change the consensus view of a phenomenon, subsequent publications can address that, but the original publication doesn't change (it can only be retracted, if it's found to be really wrong). A Wikipedia article can be updated on a moment-by-moment basis. In terms of social construction of knowledge, the more people have reviewed something, the more we can trust it. Hundreds of people continually updating a popular Wikipedia page arguably creates the most reviewed and up-to-date information source ever created."[185]

---

182 Wikipedia, "Special Statistics," accessed November 14, 2022, https://en.wikipedia.org/wiki/Special:Statistics.

183 Wikipedia, "Encyclopedia Britannica," last updated November 11, 2022, https://en.wikipedia.org/wiki/Encyclop%C3%A6dia_Britannica.

184 Natalie Wolchover, "How Accurate Is Wikipedia?," LiveScience.com, January 24, 2011, https://www.livescience.com/32950-how-accurate-is-wikipedia.html.

185 Amy S. Bruckman, Should You Believe Wikipedia? (Cambridge, England: Cambridge University Press, February 3, 2022)

The leadership question is why would a multitude of people, most of whom Wikimedia staff don't even know, commit their resources to this project? How is Jimmy Wales leading these volunteers? Consider that he may never get to meet them, yet they are contributing to the success of his project.

I must point out that I haven't yet met any of its 550 staff nor undertaken thorough research on the Wikimedia Foundation. However, based on my analysis of publicly available information, vision, transparency, and engagement may be among Wikimedia's most significant success factors. For the sake of leaders involved in collaborative projects, let's take a glance at these factors.

First, let's start with vision. At the time of this writing, the Wikimedia Foundation has a scrolling banner in several languages on its front page. It reads, "Imagine a world in which every single human being can freely share in the sum of all knowledge."[186]

Such a vision is captivating. If you want people to work for you for free, you must have a compelling vision that gives them a stake in your project. It would also help if you cultivated the ability to communicate that vision persuasively.

Second, transparency is required if you want the crowd to be involved in your cause. There is a high degree of openness at Wikimedia. For example, it has published details of the lobbyist it hired in 2011 "to lobby the United States Congress."[187] Therefore, if you want the crowd to work for you for free, please ensure you learn how to wash your garments in public and have no skeletons in your closet. For without transparency, you won't go very far.

---

186 Wikipedia Foundation, https://wikimediafoundation.org/.

187 Wikipedia, "Wikimedia Foundation," last updated November 9, 2022, https://en.wikipedia.org/wiki/Wikimedia_Foundation.

Lastly, if you want to crowdsource anything, you must find ways of engaging the public. Wikipedia organizes regular public events around the world. However, its board composition is the most unambiguous indication of its seriousness about working with the crowd. One-half of the board seats come from the community. For the remaining half, Wales has one, and the board appoints the rest.[188] That means the community has a considerable say in the strategic decisions of Wikipedia.

This new way of collaboration is rapidly growing. Its form, called crowdfunding, is used for raising money from so many people in typically small amounts. Crowdfunding is a multibillion-dollar market used to raise funds for new businesses and products, pay hospital bills, and help all different causes. Whichever creative idea you come up with in this new industry, vision, transparency, and engagement will remain important factors for the leader.

Whether adapting, collaborating, or crowdsourcing, leaders must not get carried away with success. They must remain humble.

HUMILITY

Without humility, pride takes center stage, and mistakes beam like a floodlight. The nineteenth-century English philosopher John Ruskin asserted:

> I have been more and more convinced, the more I think of it, that, in general, pride is at the bottom of all great mistakes. All other passions do occasional good; but whenever pride puts in its word, everything goes wrong;

---

188 Wikipedia, "Wikimedia Foundation."

and what it might really be desirable to do, quiet and innocently, it is normally dangerous to do proudly.[189]

In hindsight, pride has been responsible for many of my mistakes. As an unmarried person, I took risks without much caution. When I failed, I would move on without serious reflection. I carried that impulsive behavior into marriage. The first few years of marriage were frustrating, as Mhide was never excited with my rushed ideas. While living in Gabon, I conceived a risky project that would take all our savings. Of course, Mhide didn't buy into it, and I was upset.

Later that evening, I decided to convert one of our unused bedrooms into a study. Mhide suggested that I plan before making the change. Angry and defiant, I boldly went to the room to remove the bed as the first step of my assignment. Unknown to me, the bed had been nailed to the wall so I couldn't move it! Defeated and disappointed, I quietly sneaked into our bedroom. I didn't respond to Mhide, as she wanted to know why I came in so soon. I lay in bed that night thinking of the many times I had failed despite my initial excitement with new ideas.

You may think I started listening carefully to my wife after that night. Yes, I've improved over the years. Unfortunately, pride is a very stubborn companion. It doesn't leave, even when its presence becomes a nuisance. It knows that, deep inside, you still cherish it.

Please note that pride is more than a nuisance; it is destructive. It lifts you to a high plane of superiority from where you look down on others.[190] However, be careful that elevation is unstable and dangerous, as King Solomon rightly observed: "Pride goes before

---

189 J. Harry Michael Jr., *Selections from the Writings of John Ruskin, Evil of Pride* (London: Smith, Elder & Co.), 348.

190 J. Harry Michael Jr., "Deteriorating Effects of Pride," *Selections from the Writings of John Ruskin* (London: Smith, Elder & Co.), 349.

destruction, a haughty spirit before a fall" (Proverbs 16:18). Therefore, I am convinced that pride is responsible for most business failures worldwide.

Conversely, with humility, there are fewer blunders as we are attentive to discern what is helpful and what is not. Moreover, we realize we don't need to prove ourselves or show off anything to anyone. We, instead, will listen carefully to our spouses, kids, mentors, colleagues, friends, volunteers, and social media contacts, even when we don't like what they say.

Perhaps the most critical aspect of humility is acknowledging God as the Supreme Leader of the universe, who is above all. In 1 Corinthians 4:7, Apostle Paul asked, "For who makes you different from anyone else? What do you have that you did not receive? And if you did receive it, why do you boast as though you did not?"

We won't take credit for our innovations and inventions when we realize that all we are and have come from God. Instead, we will show gratitude to God for everything. We will also show appreciation to others who have contributed to our success. Without their help, yours would also be a miserable failure.

For this reason, being humble makes it much easier to lead others. In addition, in humility, when you take on a new role, you will value what others have done before your arrival.

CHAPTER 17

START!

If you know the beginning well, the end will not shock you.
—AFRICAN PROVERB

At this point, I will assume that you have read the earlier chapters and have gained a good understanding of the core ideas presented. Nevertheless, let me restate my main point here. A versatile leader is a person of integrity who, with others, creates valued outcomes using appropriate metaphors. You don't have to be a superhero to become a versatile leader. You simply need to make up your mind and then start.

I suggest you kick off your journey using the journalist metaphor to identify the urgent things. Then use the physician metaphor to gain insight into the strategic status. These two metaphors will expedite your onboarding process. The actions you take after you have found out about the existing situation are equally important. The flowchart in Figure 17.1 will guide you during the early stages of implementing the lessons from *The Versatile Leader*.

> **You don't have to be a superhero to become a versatile leader. You simply need to make up your mind and then start.**

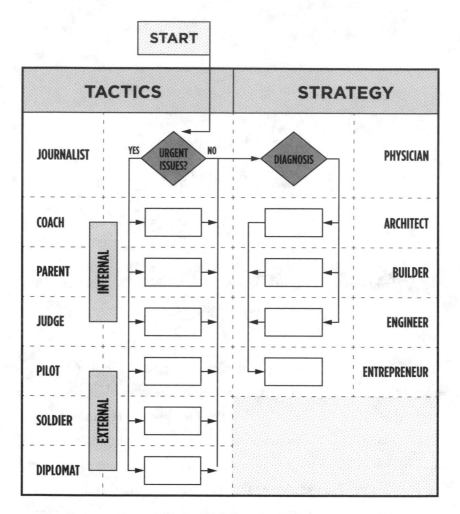

Figure 17.1: Where to start

STOP THE BLEEDING

When you get into a new situation, please use the journalist metaphor to find out if there is any urgent matter at hand. I encountered such a problem on my first day at work in Port-Gentil, Gabon, in September 1997. We had just started with the handover when I saw a fax message from our main client threatening to terminate our service contract. I asked my colleague about the situation. He said, "It's a normal complaint of a client." Not seeing anything normal about it, I immediately made that issue my priority. I studied the contract terms, the length of time the problem had been pending, and the previous attempts at solving it. Then, I took the necessary steps and fixed the six-month-old problem during my first week there.

Just like emergency workers who arrive at the scene of an accident, the new leader should do what is necessary to stop the bleeding. Reflecting on his early days as the new CEO of IBM, Louis Gerstner said, "We'd stopped the bleeding, reversed the breakup plan, and clarified IBM's basic mission. The holes in the hull had been patched. This ship was not going to sink."[191]

Therefore, when you get into a new position, you need to find out if there is a pressing issue that cannot wait. Then, please work with the relevant stakeholders and address it immediately. However, if there is no urgent problem, do not invent one. Don't dent your credibility and derail your onboarding process with pseudoemergencies.

Also, no matter what you meet upon arrival, I caution you not to make changes too hastily. Starting in a new position and implementing the wrong changes will ruin trust. Moreover, two stable states are involved in a change—the initial and final states. If you don't understand the prevailing condition, your change will likely end in disarray.

Suppose you have been part of the organization already. In that case, you may know many things at the beginning of your new assignment. In this case, you can hit the ground running, like Joshua. As the Bible indicates, Joshua had been working with Moses for decades. Moses was also meticulous and left a clear plan before he died. Joshua's first speech as the new leader of the nation of Israel contained instructions to his assistants: "Go through the camp and tell the people, 'Get your provisions ready. Three days from now you will cross the

---

191   Louis V. Gerstner Jr., *Who Says Elephants Can't Dance?*.

Jordan here to go in and take possession of the land the Lord your God is giving you for your own.'"[192]

After hearing this, the nation willingly followed Joshua's instructions and crossed the River Jordan to the other side!

Even if you can issue orders like Joshua, you must be careful. Avoid what happened to Executive Order 13769, issued by Donald Trump during his early days as the president of the United States. The "Trump travel ban," as it's commonly called, faced many protests, was blocked by the courts, and had to be replaced.[193]

Michael Watkins, the author of *The First 90 Days*, noted:

> Far too many new leaders don't effectively diagnose their situations and tailor their strategies accordingly. Then, because they don't understand the situation, they make unnecessary mistakes. This painful cycle happens because people usually model their transitions on a limited set of experiences.[194]

Therefore, you should diagnose before making any significant decisions.

DIAGNOSE

Using the physician metaphor to diagnose your new organization would be necessary. Before even taking vital signs, doctors ascertain some basic facts, such as the age and sex of the patient. In the same way, a leader needs to know their new organization's place on the S-Curve (see chapter 3) and its industry. For example, an oil and gas

---

192   Joshua 1:11.

193   Wikipedia, "Executive Order 13769," last updated November 13, 2022, https://en.wikipedia.org/wiki/Executive_Order_13769.

194   Michael Watkins, The First 90 Days Quicklet (Singapore: PatridgePublishers, December 1, 2021)

exploration venture may take several years before reaching a break-even point. In contrast, a consulting firm may achieve it in months. So understanding the nature of the business and its industry is essential to your diagnosis.

How long will it take to complete the initial diagnosis? It depends on several factors: first, the stage of the organization on the S-Curve; second, the complexity of the situation; and third, what you already know before your first day in the new position.

Suppose you are appointed to create an organization from scratch, like Joseph in Egypt. In that case, your starting point is at the very beginning of the S-Curve. The only thing existing before your involvement is a dream or an idea that may not even be yours. Yet you have the responsibility to bring it to reality. Please find out what resources you have initially, the extent of your authority, the expected outcome, and the timeline required to deliver. Once you've grasped your new organization well, the architect will be your primary metaphor to drive your leadership strategy. Use it to make plans suitable to the preparation stage we covered in chapter 3.

If it is an existing organization, you need to find out how long it has existed. If you realize it is still new, it is most likely a start-up. Start-ups usually lack structure, yet they can do without it initially. Don't expect a positive net income at an early stage of a start-up. The founder, investors, or loans are the sources of cash for most start-ups. A healthy start-up clearly understands the problem it is trying to solve and has a vision for the future. It also understands the market's willingness to adopt its offerings. It will be necessary to obtain all the information from various stakeholders as early as possible.

That brings us to an important question: How do you know if your organization is in a growth stage? An organization in a growth stage has already passed the break-even point. There is a demand for its products. The vision is understood and implemented. Yet the structure, processes, and procedures are weak or nonexistent. Once your diagnosis shows the growth stage, you will need the builder metaphor to take the organization to its full potential. As explained in chapter 6, builders need to understand the vision, history, and success factors. Then they need to work hard to take it to the next level.

If you build well, your company will eventually reach maturity. A builder may still do well at the early stage of maturity. However, the result may not be the same as during the growth stage. Over time, the growth rate will slow down.

A mature organization is the hardest to change. Therefore, when you enter a mature organization, you must be careful about how you go about your preconceived plans. Tactically, the diplomat metaphor should be your daily companion. Strategically, you will need a combination of builder and engineer metaphors.

Suppose you join the company when it is obviously in decline. Where should you start? First, you still need the physician metaphor to find out if this is true and what is the likely cause of the decline. Then, once you have confirmed the company's status, you will need the engineer metaphor to guide your turnaround strategy.

As you can see in Figure 17.1, no matter the state of the organization or the metaphor you use as your initial strategy, you must deliver results. For that, you need the entrepreneur metaphor. Please create KPIs, which you will use to track your progress.

In your new role, there are things you will like naturally and others that will be a struggle. Please delegate if you have capable hands around you. If, for any reason, you can't delegate, then you need to act like an entrepreneur. Entrepreneurs want results to the extent that they are willing to take on any role, even if they don't find it pleasant. Furthermore, your ability to work seamlessly with others will be required for you to deliver good results.

EXAMPLE

Here's a story that illustrates the key points in this chapter. The characters and names of companies are not real, unlike all the others in this book.

DeziBanker was founded in Egypt in 2010 as a financial inclusion solution that helps banks reach rural areas without the need for creating traditional branches. DeziBanker expanded rapidly to Brazil, Indonesia, India, Nigeria, China, the US, and Angola.

In early 2018, Miss Ana Bonga, an Angolan citizen, joined Dezi-Banker in Silicon Valley, California, straight after her studies. She is an excellent software programmer. She became a team leader after barely one year in the company. Subsequently, she was transferred to the headquarters in Cairo.

Please note that the Angolan subsidiary was created in 2017 and has grown to fifty full-time employees working in their office in Talatona, a suburb of Luanda. Banco Breeze, a leading commercial bank in Angola, contracted DeziBanker to help it expand banking services to rural communities in Angola. Unfortunately, DeziBanker Angola is struggling to cope with the demands of the new project. Despite her limited experience, the directors considered Ana their best choice to lead their business in Angola. She was excited to return home after nearly ten years abroad. However, her lack of management experience worried Ana.

Upon arrival in Angola in the middle of 2019, Ana started with the journalist metaphor. While being introduced to the staff, she asked questions, listened, and took notes. On her third day, she decided to visit Banco Breeze. An angry client greeted Ana. Two months after the contract, no one in DeziBanker could tell them when the project would start!

Back in the office, Ana probed to find out why there was a delay. The software developers blamed the project manager, who in turn accused procurement. Lastly, procurement said it was the finance manager's fault. Consequently, the relationship between the departments soured.

Ana knew that if the blame game continued, progress would be impossible. Exercising her authority and calling the managers to order was a temptation she resisted because she was still very new. Instead, using the diplomat metaphor, she acted as a mediator between her new colleagues. After hours of "peace talk," the managers agreed to end the blame game. They immediately started working productively for the company's best interest.

Ana then resumed her trace of the other issues that were causing delays. It turned out that getting approvals from the head office took weeks due to communication and logistics challenges. Each time a document had to be signed, the original and translated copy had to be sent by courier to Cairo. After signing, they sent them back similarly. Sometimes, it would take three weeks to complete the process.

Ana was candid when she called the head office. She requested authorization to be the legal representative of the company immediately. Otherwise, it would be impossible to execute the contract with Banco Breeze. Moreover, the entire subsidiary was in jeopardy because of administrative bottlenecks. Fortunately, they approved her request, so she started operating independently. As a result, she acquired all the hardware needed for the project, and the developers commenced work.

Ana continued with her initial diagnosis using the physician metaphor. Three months later, she concluded that DeziBanker Angola was a start-up struggling to transition to growth stage. She used the builder as her primary metaphor to drive the growth process. While creating processes and structures for growth, Ana guided the team to deploy the Banco Breeze project to one hundred rural communities successfully.

After three years in her role, DeziBanker Angola was recognized as the best-performing subsidiary worldwide. Despite COVID-19, the revenue in Angola went up 400 percent in two years, and net profit grew proportionally. Miss Ana Bonga received the Best Manager of the Year 2022 award. In her acceptance speech at the company headquarters in Cairo, Ana said:

> Today, I'm honored and humbled to receive this award on behalf of the DeziBanker staff and other stakeholders in Angola. Three years ago, I was nervous without management training or experience and almost declined to take such a visible role. I'm grateful to God for sending Mrs. Angela Malek my way.
>
> It happened that I sat next to Angela on my return flight to Cairo from Addis Ababa. It was unexpected that I talked to this stranger about the offer I needed to respond to the following week. When we landed, Angela

gave me this book [Ana now raised her hand and waved the book]. I read *The Versatile Leader*, became confident, and looked forward to the new challenge.

To my surprise, the reality I met on arrival in Angola was worse than I had anticipated. Many of you here may remember how Banco Breeze threatened to abandon the project. Indeed, everyone worked hard to get the project back on track. There's one who deserves special mention here. It is our driver, Mr. Antonio Dondo. The equipment arrived at the airport, and customs clearance was a considerable challenge. Antonio chased the process in customs every day for three weeks. Eventually, his persistence paid off, and he got the equipment out! That is just one example of the commitment of our people that made this achievement possible. I'm so proud to be part of a team like this.

Summing up everything, the flowchart of DeziBanker's example looks like this:

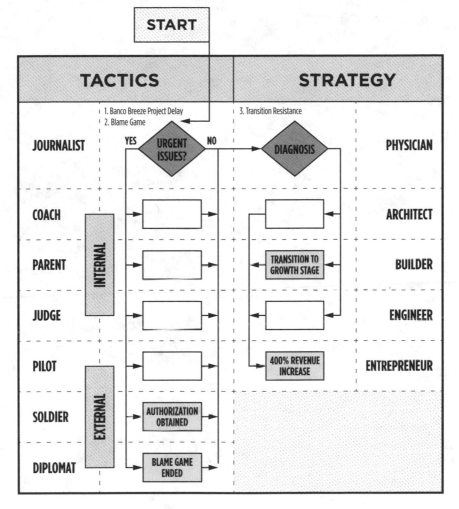

Figure 17.2: Where to start: Ana Bonga

Finally, I want to congratulate you on your perseverance. "All good things must come to an end," goes the popular saying. But your leadership journey shouldn't end here. Now go ahead and lead with excellence. The world is desperately seeking versatile leaders like you.

ABOUT THE AUTHOR

When Msuega Tese was growing up in a rural Nigerian village, his father would allow him to sit within hearing distance of the elders' (community leaders') discussions. These conversations greatly impacted how Tese thinks about life, relationships, and business.

After more than a decade working for a multinational oil and gas services company, in 2005, Tese cofounded Integrated Solutions Angola (ISA), where he serves as executive director.

ISA provides IT services for leading enterprise customers in Angola. It is well known for its sound business principles and practices. In addition, it has an unsullied track record of deploying and maintaining complex technology solutions.

Tese also has business interests in other countries, such as Nigeria, Uganda, Tanzania, and United Arab Emirates.

He is passionate about finding practical ways to help others learn, understand, and practice leadership. As a lifelong student of leadership, Tese offers readers a fresh perspective independent of popular views. As a devout Christian, he finds inspiration from his relationship with the God of the Bible.

Tese graduated with an honors degree in electrical engineering from the University of Port Harcourt, Nigeria. He also took part in the Owner/President Management program of the Harvard Business School.

Tese is married to Mhide. Together they have five children.

GET IN TOUCH

WWW.MSUEGATESE.COM

EMAIL: ME@MSUEGATESE.COM